OVERACHIEVING AF

Overachieving Failure & The Lessons It Teaches

Copyright © 2020 Connie Chi

All rights reserved.

ISBN: 9798657316889

Connie Chi

ACKNOWLEDGEMENT

It is with profound thanks from the bottom of my heart to my fellow female entrepreneurs who dare to venture into the world of the unknown in order to make the world a better place. I deeply admire and respect your achievements, grit, and ingenuity that continue to inspire us this lifetime while paving the way for new innovators in the marketplace.

SPECIAL THANKS

With tremendous gratitude, thanks, and appreciation to my mom who continues to challenge me to overachieve greatness. My dad who had given me the greatest gift, teaching me the power and true worth of unconditional love. Thank you for the honor to have loved you without limitations. Joe Polish for his unforgettable guidance and authentic kindness during my darkest moment in life and business.

Ariel Lopez, founder of Knac for always championing my entrepreneurial spirit for over a decade. Sergio Delavicci, actor in John Wick 3 for his friendship and support throughout the years. Thank you for writing a beautifully profound foreword for this book. There are countless others to thank and much too long to list, but for those I've missed please know that I hold a massive amount of love and gratitude for each of you in my heart.

CONTENTS

Foreword

Introduction

Part 1: Lessons That No One Taught You

Part 2: Dream Like No One's Looking

Part 3: Dirty Secrets of Overachievers

Overachieving Final Thoughts

About The Author

FOREWORD

We live in a very cold world. It's something we often hear people say around us. But the truth is we live in the type of world that we create for ourselves. We can be our own biggest and worst enemy. As long as we're alive we have choices, options, and decisions. Everything starts within ourselves. Unfortunately as much as we like to blame others and hold them accountable for our own failure, we can't blame anyone else for our failures but our own selves. The truth is we can be our own biggest limitation. The opinion we form about ourselves can sometimes become our reality.

I believe that everything in this universe is made out of energy. The kind of energy that can only be determined by our thoughts and actions. We get back from the universe what we put out there. With all of that being said self doubt is worse than failure will ever be.

Hard work beats talent if there is no hard work behind talent. You have to constantly work on yourself and invest time in self-development. This is not an easy route but it can be very rewarding and worthwhile. In order to be successful in life, don't be afraid to fail.

Enjoy the book. It will change the way you look at the world.

-Sergio Delavicci

"Ruska Roma" (Ermolai)

Actor in John Wick 3

INTRODUCTION

In writing this book I wanted to share with you some of my most valuable lessons as an overachiever. Many people have always asked me how did you become so successful at accomplishing so much. I think it's something that's been instilled in me at a young age. My mother employed the typical Asian "Tiger Mom" parenting skills. She forced me to think for myself, nothing was good enough, figure it out, and that there's an answer to what you want in life. You know at the time it truly pissed me off because I had wished my mom was more affectionate. But as I've gotten older I've learned to appreciate those lessons.

Even though those lessons were hard, it set the gold standard for me on my personal journey into adulthood. It gave me the tools and gusto to courageously chase my dreams. It also taught me to embrace my inner rebel that wasn't afraid to put myself out there. When we have that unshakeable belief that we can accomplish the craziest things in the world we actually do. Isn't that something?

Today in some way I wonder if we are raising a generation of ill-equipped, over-sensitive children? Or have we as a society completely accepted that it's no longer about figuring things out in life. Have we lost our way? I say this because my mom's parenting style though very traditionally old school seems to be shunned upon. There's all these new rules about how and what to say to your kids that I wished was around when I was growing up.

The key to being a successful overachiever is to have a balance. Balance in our life lessons learned, our dreams, and the skills we need to acquire to continuously charge forward relentlessly. It's not just about the wins but it's also about our losses and what we do in those darkest moments when no one is looking. Are we actively self shaming or being present? All these are questions to think about as you continue forward.

I want you to know that each of my successes and businesses in life we're born out of personal heartbreaks, pain, and massive disappointments. Every single time I was sad, heartbroken or just felt like I wasn't good enough, I'd venture out to start a new business, new project, and somehow it worked for me. Relationship breakups were the best motivators for me to level up my business chops.

In no way am I glorifying entrepreneurship because it takes a very special kind of person to endure just the emotional aspect of it. It can torment you or bring you a sense of undeniable freedom that no amount of money can buy. For me I build businesses to chase my dreams and utilize my experience to help the next generation to courageously chase theirs.

The lessons I share with you are from my own personal experiences; it doesn't mean what you're experiencing is any less. Instead I welcome you to take whatever lessons you'd like from my personal journey. As every piece will not be a fit for you at the moment. So let's do this, let's overachieve failure!

PART 1: LESSONS THAT NO ONE TAUGHT YOU

Here's the deal and I'm not going to sugar coat it for you- no one will teach you how to live. Matter of fact none of us came into this world with a personal manual listing out the steps of life that says, "If you do this and that happens then proceed to index B for further instructions."

So why is it that we are compulsively, maybe even obsessively looking for the imaginary blueprint and hacks of life? Could it be that we're so conditioned to follow the rules, that we lost our way? Or maybe social media has set the golden seal of standard when it comes to what life should look like.

Real talk- there's no secret map to life and you definitely don't get any prizes for finishing first. Look no one is going to live your life for you, we're all born with the freedom of choice. The ability to formulate our own paths, harvest our own wins and take in our losses. I'm not saying life is a game of win or lose, but it sure does feel great when we're winning. What exactly then are the lessons that no one bothers to clue us in on? I think the better question to ask is what's the real conversation that you never about when it comes to overachieving.

LESSON 1: IMPERFECT AF

Perfection is a dirty word that so many of us fall prey to.

Yes, yes we've all heard the raging mantra that no one's perfect but do we really believe that? I mean women and men want to look perfect to attract the right person in their life. Parents want to be perfect parents in order to raise perfect children who follow directions and have impeccable manners. Children want to be perfect for parents and the cycle continues to perpetuate and spill over into every area of life. Is this really the right way to live? Whatever happened to just being curious and exploring?

This was definitely not one of those lessons my parents gave me. Growing up exploration wasn't really encouraged. Matter of fact it was seen as breaking ranks, dangerous and even the downfall of the family honor because it meant you were imperfect. I was raised in New York City, proud to say I'm a true NYC girl-raised by the concrete jungle as Alicia Keys sings in her song. If you've ever been to NYC you'll know that it's truly one of those cities that's filled with endless exploration options.

In the 80's NYC wasn't as chic as it is today filled with vegan restaurants, bougie sidewalk cafes, $10 coffees, and gluten-free menus. It was definitely not a number one pick when it comes to raising a family. Matter of fact I grew up in a neighborhood that was known for the heroine. So to keep my brother and I off the streets and away from gangs, my parents like any typical Asian parents enrolled us in a ton of extracurricular activities. Piano and violin lessons were a must. Art lessons, Kumon math, and reading classes on weekdays and weekends were dedicated to Chinese school and religion classes. At a young age, we were set up to play what's called a, "solo sport," activities that can be mastered alone. Not just mastered alone but perfectly mastered alone.

With a schedule like that, there wasn't much room for exploration or making new friends. Looking back I think this was probably where most of my challenges for relationship building stem from. I got so used to being perfectly self-sufficient and an independent operating machine that I really didn't know the importance of a team. Nor the value of honoring my own emotions.

As a toddler I was extremely curious, even today as an adult I have this insatiable curiosity to understand why and how things work. There was a time when I was about three years old that I developed the habit of rummaging through people's things, personal boundaries wasn't a concept on my radar. It started with going through all the drawers in the house and then it spilled over into going through the things of other family members.

During my childhood, I was fortunate enough to have had the chance to travel a lot. My grandmother owned elite private schools all over Taipei and my mom would travel back and forth between the states and Taiwan. I was raised by my grandmother, great grandmother, and many aunts and uncles while my father worked tirelessly in the restaurant business. They say it takes a tribe to raise a child and I couldn't agree more with that.

I had a favorite aunt in Taiwan and at the time she was single and loved kids. She'd spoil all the kids in the family by buying us new clothes and taking us out to eat at the night market. The Taiwanese night market is filled with all sorts of delicious food from savory, salty and sweet. You eat finger foods off a stick or soup noodles out of a plastic bag, to oyster filled pancakes and all sorts of shaved ice. You could go from vendor to vendor tasting snacks as you walked around the most aromatic market.

Or if you wanted to "dine-in" some vendors would set up plastic chairs and tables for customers right on the streets. The night market was nothing swanky it's as you expected, streets lined with vendors open at all hours of the night. There were even retail stores, some had actual dedicated brick and mortar space. While others were simply a mosh of whatever they were selling sprawled on a cloth placed on the ground. You could probably get anything cheap here.

It was definitely the happening nightlife in Taiwan and it also housed a lot of my aunt's favorite spots to shop while she haggled most of the owners for a discount. She was my very first teacher when it comes to negotiations. I would watch her talk down the shop owners to the point where they would just give up and honor her demands. It was mesmerizing to watch how one person who is 4 feet 5 inches tall can convince another to abandon their pricing. I was impressed!

My aunt's negotiation skills awarded her the most fashionably forward auntie in the family. She always had cool new colorful clothes, her hair was always professionally done, makeup done to perfection and colorful heels that matches every outfit she owned.

One afternoon left to my own devices, wandering around my favorite aunt's office at the private school, I discovered the beauty of makeup. My little hands rummaged through each drawer pulling out lipsticks and eyeshadows and this was the exact moment that my inner artist was unleashed. As I pulled off the caps of her lipstick, I realized that each stick was a different color and it could be used like crayons. My face and white-washed walls of the office turned into the canvas for what became a menagerie of lipstick Piccaso masterpieces. Needless to say, I was quite satisfied with my creation.

Unfortunately, the adults weren't as pleased, my mother especially was horrified that I took my curiosity to new heights and for that, I was punished, forced to kneel on the floor while being scolded.

I remembered as a kid I was punished a lot, spankings and time outs seemed like a regular occurrence. To me, this translated into you're not perfect so you're going to be punished for it and being curious is a punishable offense. But this didn't stop me from wondering what the world was made of.

When I was in grade school, living in a one-bedroom apartment in New York City, my brother and I would always see ants scrambling across the windowsill during the summer. We both wondered where these ants were coming from and where they were going and if there was a way to stop them. Kids being kids, we thought about gluing ants to the windowsill. We both pulled out our Elmers glue and started to squirt them onto the ants.

I'll admit looking back at it, it was quite vile of us to even think of such an act. Our scheme of gluing ants to the windowsill was a summer pastime that resulted in every window in the apartment lined with a trail of glue frozen ants, a permanent windowsill decoration that drove my mom nuts. This was the very reason she started buying us stick glue as part of our back to school supplies.

In our family, perfection was the foundation of so many things whether it was piano lessons, tests in school, or even simple art assignments. There was no room for error. This was probably the derivative of the sheer fact that my parents came to the United States with nothing and only wanted to give us kids a great life.

They wanted to set us up for ultimate success. To them, it was simply about working hard to achieve perfection so that the rest of the world wouldn't have the opportunity to tear us down. In the process, it taught us to have thick skin. There were countless moments that I remember wanting to give up whether it was the piano or Chinese lessons and mom would always say to me, "you get up exactly where you fall down and do it again and again until you do it without thinking."

Growing up being perfect was extremely painful, I struggled a lot with my happiness and at the time not knowing how to ascertain it. I was frustrated because I knew that this wasn't an enjoyable way to live life. Yet I didn't know how to express my own desires. I took a lot of my frustrations out on the piano, that was the only way I knew how to express myself without words. It's as if I was an emotional mute trying desperately to let the world know I was in pain.

The detriment of perfection is simply this- we become so challenged at not only expressing our emotional needs but it also breeds the incapacity to accept failure when things don't happen the way you intend.

All the way up to my late 20's I had a very difficult time accepting failure and mishaps. It wasn't something I was well equipped for. Receiving my first F in college was the hardest lesson in imperfection. I remembered I cried when I saw that F plastered across my end of semester report. It was a detrimental blow, not just to my ego but everything I was taught.

For the first time in my life I was imperfect, and now what do I do? All these emotions came up and all I could think of was how do I tell my parents? Well that first F, I got over it and continued on to get 2 more

F's. It wasn't as bad after getting over the initial shock of, "how could I of all people get an F."

Then came the first time I got fired from a job. This was another blow to perfection, I won't lie, I was pissed. How could a company fire me? When I shared this with a friend of mine I remembered he told me, "Connie we're all expendable." Naturally, that wasn't something I wanted to hear, instead, I vowed to figure out a way to make myself not so easily expendable.

The first experience of anything isn't always going to be the best, but with practice, you end up getting it right. And practice I did, because in my lifetime I think I must've gotten fired 5 times from corporate jobs. Not many people would proudly announce that. But to me, it was my glory. It was my way of being perfectly rebellious and let me tell you after being fired so many times I've mastered the art of getting fired. I confess, I might've coached a few disgruntled office mates on how to get fired too. Yes, I was and probably still am an employer's worst nightmare.

Perfection will be the best teacher, it teaches you discipline but it numbs your ability to explore your emotional palette. In some ways in order to be perfect you need to shut out your doubts, the what if's, and the worry in order to have this laser focus, and robotic execution. In ways, I'm grateful that perfection was drilled into me at a young age because it taught me to operate on a high level. But the dangerous part about perfection is that you can easily get stuck in that space.

Expecting that everything you do will be perfect is one of the biggest unrealistic expectations you can have on yourself. Life is filled with surprises and moments that you never planned for. With age I've learned to accept the concept of being perfectly imperfect. It's a hard one to embrace but like anything else the more you experience it the quicker you rebound from it.

What's interesting was that I once heard someone say that your imperfect work is someone else's perfect work. If you think about it, it makes a lot of sense. When we've walked through the fire and experienced the rainbow of outcomes from our achievements it's easier to see what's imperfect to us. But for someone else who's just starting out on their journey, your imperfections look a whole lot like what they dream of.

I remembered when I was starting my speaking career I was invited for the first time ever to speak on stage at the Javits Center. This is THE largest event space in all of New York City and it's the place that all events with a major bankroll hold their events.

This was the first time ever I was going to be on stage, none the less at this massive space. I practiced my presentation every day for 6 months and I felt like I knew my presentation inside out. When it came time to deliver, my body shook and I was sweating like crazy. While on stage my nose was running, I was struggling to maintain a tone that didn't reflect my nervousness. As I stood on that stage and looked out into the lights I saw close to 200 pairs of eyeballs staring back ready to take in every word that came out of my mouth.

I was overwhelmed but needed to deliver, so here it went. As I was about 25 minutes into my presentation, my slides stopped appearing on the screen. I was flying blind-completely blind. My first presentation with close to 200 people and I was like a deer in headlights. Luckily I memorized all of my slides in order to continue on. Needless to say, I don't think I stopped sweating on that stage.

Here's where things get interesting after I was done speaking, person after person came up to me to tell me how great it was! They even wanted to work with my company! In my head, I thought to myself, "really me? You want to work with me after that presentation?" This was what solidified the fact for me that my idea of perfection is solely doctrine up. Here are a bunch of people who thought I had value. That was how my speaking career was launched!

I've learned in life that things will always be imperfect, if you're spending time on perfection you'll never rally the courage to actually take action. Isn't that what life is really about? Exploration, results and endless lessons. Before starting my first business I spent close to 5 years trying to "perfect" it before entering into the business arena and 6 months researching all the contingency backup strategie if my business failed.

Personally if I could redo that moment I wouldn't have waited five years. It was pointless because nothing went as planned. The honest truth is that my own inaction was born out of one thing and one thing only. THE FEAR OF FAILING.

Yes, that fear which plagues many of us and it's the thing that nicely goes hand in hand with perfection. Two evil cousins that will stop you dead in your tracks and have your brain playing out all sorts of scenarios that probably would never happen. I spent $30K in a year on online courses, looking for validation that it was okay to be imperfect.

Funny thing, I never got that validation. In fact I got the same reassurance from all those who have tread the murky waters of entrepreneurship before me, "you will never be ready, entrepreneurship is about failing and testing till you find a way that works for you." So if you want perfect, then I'd suggest finding yourself a corporate job. One that is perfectly set up and all you need to do is show up and show out the results.

The more imperfections that presented itself in my day to day life the more it felt like I was actually making progress. Can you imagine the irony of that? When I finally embraced imperfection in my career or in my personal life the more I started to feel like life was limitless. It's a possibility that I never imagined and with all this room for exploration where do you actually start?

I finally realized that all this time I've underestimated my own abilities to be resilient, to be courageous and my willingness to open up to the unknown. Was the process scary? I'll say it is a beautiful moment to come to this acceptance. But I was scared because imperfection was something that textbooks and family would never talk about. Back then when I was growing up you didn't have access to information the way you do today. Not everything was Google-able. In fact if you wanted information you would go to the library and check out a book.

The point is this…

If you're so busy chasing the image of perfection and we do this our entire life, we miss out on essentially everything in life.

For many years I chased the elusive perfection, matter of fact I played the perfection game so well that it became my sole form of oxygen. Everything I did had to be perfect from employee to daughter that I lost track of who I was. My own happiness was so far forgotten that if you asked me what made me happy 20 years ago? The answer would have been a simple head cocked to the side looking at you as though you spoke a foreign language.

At the same time I'd go into my mental rolodex to find the perfect words to string together that would be the ideal answer that people equated to self happiness. Heck you ask me that question today, it's one clear answer- chasing my dreams like a madwoman. I want to feel that feeling of pure bliss and freedom to design my life the way I intend to and feel the way I want to.

It took a lot of self inventory to get to a point where you can clearly articulate an authentic answer that's yours. Trust me I know. Being perfect all the time you lose your identity and eventually become just a dried outer shell wondering if there's more to life. Perfection is when we look in the mirror.

LESSON 2: PEOPLE PLEASING SUCKS

Slow it down a few notches with the people-pleasing. I get it, who doesn't want to be liked, loved and accepted for who they are? But going about it by simply pleasing everyone is more detrimental to you. Greatness isn't accomplished by being someone else's doormat or "yes man," in fact it'll be the quickest way to allow people to disrespect you. Learn to hold grace for yourself and set standards.

Standards are the polite public boundaries that we let the world know what we will and will not accept. I promise you it'll change as you grow and learn. I'm sure what you were willing to tolerate and accept in your youth you'd probably wouldn't even give it a breath of air today.

For me, it was really easy to fall into the trap of people-pleasing, especially family members, that's what I was taught. You do EVERYTHING for your parents- your family. What's so fraught with that mentality is that you become an enabler of not just bad behavior but sparing our parents the opportunity for growth. Matter of fact I see it as an injustice in many ways. An injustice first to them because if you love someone you'd want to see them grow and flourish. The second injustice is of course to yourself, you hinder your own growth when you become unwilling to change your blueprint in order to fit into theirs.

We all know that if we're not growing, not learning, that we're in fact dying and it's wholeheartedly true. Nourishing ourselves not just with the sustenance of growth but also with openness is to do so holds space for miracles to happen.

People pleasing can become an addiction, chasing a high our brain gets from it feels great. It's being fed a "drug" that essentially is activating neurons and releasing chemicals that for some bring euphoria or even ecstasy. My people-pleasing addiction had gotten so bad that when I realized I needed to give up the feel-good drug I was already deeply angry at the world. More so I was angry at myself for allowing this to get so far as it did- over 2 decades to be exact.

This deeply rooted addiction stems from desperately wanting to be loved. My childhood wasn't filled with a lot of physical affection or emotional affection either so people pleasing fed this tremendous need for validation. It got so bad for me that it was the exact thing that kept me in damaging relationships to the point where I had almost lost my life.

It wasn't easy to look in the mirror and really understand what and why this happens. Truth is, it's always easier to blame others for things that go array or just don't fit into your ideal perfect life. But what's the point of playing victim if you never learn the lessons and keep repeating it over and over again. I call this our spiritual homework. Each of us has different sets of personal assignments and some don't get to finish it all in one lifetime.

When it comes to extreme people-pleasers, I want you all to know that no matter how PERFECT you are at pleasing the world there will always be someone who doesn't like you. So why not like yourself first before expecting others to like you.

I remembered that being in grade school I was bullied a lot and learned quickly that if I turned into a people pleaser I wouldn't be bullied. Instead what I didn't understand as a kid was that what I was practicing was a form of self-bullying. A form that probably left a huge emotional scar that challenges the way I build relationships with people.

Once I entered into the workforce I quickly learned that people-pleasing in corporate doesn't quite work in your favor. You end up piled up with all the work that no one wants to do. Needless to say my time from high school to corporate was probably the most unhappiest time of my life.

Not only was people-pleasing my drug of choice but it also slowed me down. Every move, every decision I made was spent doubly analyzing reanalyzing and considering everyone else's feelings. How would people react if I did this or that? By people I mean every single direct member of my family. It was an exhausting exhumation of scenario after scenario that involved everyone but me.

Here's the deal when we quit pleasing others who are used to being accommodated by us, they will look at you as if you're being selfish and HELL YA! You're being selfish because without healthy boundaries we tend to lose ourselves. Matter of fact it's pretty much a guarantee. There's nothing wrong with helping people or giving them your time and energy but there needs to be a limit or healthy exchange of energy.

If you keep giving and giving without replenishing yourself then in the long run what'll happen is that you end up having nothing to give. I used to be that person who would give my entire soul to my significant other to the point where I started to resent them. I never took a real honest look at myself and eventually I was burnt out. Burnt out from relationships and burnt out from consistently over-giving.

I remembered watching a lot of my female friends growing up who seem to have this ease about setting boundaries. I'll admit, deep down I secretly wished that I too possessed the skills they did. I'd spend so much time talking to them and really studying up on how to set healthy boundaries. It wasn't until my 30's that I started to get the hang of it and understand how to set boundaries without feeling guilty.

Growing up I was guilted about everything including feeling guilty about feeling guilty if that even makes any sense. I felt guilty about not being pretty enough, smart enough, patient enough, whatever you can think of my mom guilted me for in my adolescent years. At one point I even felt guilty about not being a people pleaser. Trust me it's definitely no fun living in that state and not even realizing how much damage it's doing to yourself.

So people-pleasing is a dangerous game, one that if rules aren't set in place you can easily fall trap to a vicious cycle that ends up overlapping in every area of life. Until you start to recognize that you are the one doing it and that only you can change it, then you will constantly relive it.

LESSON 3: EXCUSES DON'T BUY HAPPINESS

Lie to yourself enough times you end up believing it. I want you to take a minute and think about this and we can use a really simple everyday example. Let's talk dating before I dive into this one, just a disclaimer: I'm by far a love expert or relationship coach but I do get asked a lot for relationship advice for some reason. But I digress.

Dating is something that's pretty much universal and most of us have experienced it. Say you really like the person you're dating and oftentimes when you call this person they tell you, "Sorry, I can't talk, I'm busy." If they say this to you enough times eventually you're going to start believing their statement less and less. Ultimately it'll probably end up with some sort of argument and both sides are left feeling not so lovey-dovey.

Now imagine you do this to yourself every time you make an excuse for whatever it is in your life. Essentially you're spending more time coming up with fabricated stories and excuses rather than finding out what will make you happy.

Our happiness is our own responsibility. Too often we're so afraid to find out what makes us happy that we use other people as our crutch for happiness. Look people aren't perfect and they won't be able to deliver happiness all the time because we have moments in life that we're happy, sad, angry and all the emotions in between. Depending on others for your happiness is not a guaranteed formula people will disappoint you, it's part of life.

Truly we all have excuses about why we're not happy, "I'm just not a happy person. It's the other person's fault for not doing things for me," and the list goes on and on. Eventually, we tell ourselves these fabricated stories long enough that we start to weave it into our blueprint of life, that we believe these excuses. I'm going to tell you point-blank that happiness is a choice. Plain and simple.

We get to choose to be happy or miserable. Some of us are happy in misery, I'm not judging. That's ok too. But most of us want better for ourselves, we all came into the world with dreams and goals. Some of us have massively lofty goals which is GREAT! If you're here reading this book it means you definitely have tremendous goals to make a better life for yourself and I applaud you for having the courage to do so.

When we stop handing the keys to our happiness to someone else or something else it's the precise moment that we start to curate something magical. We get to live life on our terms. I'm not saying that life is always going to be rainbows and unicorns, what I am saying is you get to choose the perception of any situation in life.

I too needed this reminder and one time during the holidays I got just that. As an entrepreneur, the one person, and I call him a person because I spend the most amount of time with him. My fur baby Mickey. This little eight-pound furry four-legged creature, "*my dog*" has seen me at my worst and at my best. We talk about a lot of things together, more like I talk he listens- well most of the time.

Mickey has this really bizarre habit of going nuts in the backseat whenever I take him to the gas station. For some reason, he loses his mind, all sense and sensibility goes out the window. He barks at the gas attendants the entire time the car is filling up with gas. As a pet parent, it's highly embarrassing and not to mention frustrating because I feel like I've failed at being a model pet parent. Mickey's bark is so loud that everyone at the station turns to look at him. Every time this happens I have to apologize to the attendants on Mickey's behalf between telling him the car needs a drink and screaming at him to STOP!

Normally the attendants will politely smile or laugh and say, "it's ok." I, on the other hand, spend the entire time deeply ashamed because I know this is not ok and if Caesar "*The Dog Whisperer*" saw this he would definitely not approve of this kind of behavior. Truth be told, gas station runs with Mickey in the backseat always brings me through a moment of panic and extra prayers.

Even though I saw Mickey's gas station outbursts as deeply shameful, the attendant said to me, "It's ok, your dog is just talking to me. We're having a conversation through the glass. He's cute!" At that moment I thought to myself, "WOW! What a beautiful way of looking at this situation." I experienced the outbursts as one way while the gas attendant who's standing in the cold with no gloves or a hat is looking at this as a mini conversation with my pet. To this day Mickey and I haven't mastered gas station trips, we're still both a work in progress.

The outcome of how you feel is how you look at situations in life. The same applies to happiness if you're always looking for happiness then that's going to magnify consistently in your life. You've got to believe that life is conspiring for you not against you at any given situation. I get it, it's easier sometimes to focus on the negative when it's right in front of you. But that's what most of the world does, look at news outlets, things they report on are predominantly about war, death, lack of, and so on. That's exactly why I don't watch the news, read a newspaper or even own a television.

Consciously choosing to surround yourself with things, situations and people that make you happy is the key. Initially, it can be hard if you're used to being in negativity. But just start small. That's why so many people talk about being grateful. Gratitude goes a long way matter of fact it's the mother's milk to happiness.

As someone who's running a business, it might look on the outside that I have it all. The press mentions, books, TEDx talk, and traveling to go speak. But here's the thing I still spend every morning being grateful. I start with five things and some days it's simple things like I'm grateful to have another day that I'm breathing, I'm grateful for Mickey being alive, grateful I had great sleep, and the list goes on.

If you find yourself unhappy then it's time to take an honest look at how you're looking at life. It's time you throw away your proverbial glasses, they don't work anymore! I know it sounds scary but here's the thing, it's an opportunity. What if you threw out your glasses that don't work and got a pair that allows you to see things beautifully. Here's the BEST part, IT'S DAMN NEAR FREE to change your proverbial glasses and you can change them as many times as you'd like this lifetime!

What brought you happiness ten months ago may not bring you the same level of happiness today and that's totally fine. It means you're growing as a person so KUDOS to you. Unhappiness, failures, and mistakes are all opportunities in disguise. Each moment that you were unhappy, failed or made mistakes it's an opportunity to dig deep and learn from it in order to make the next experience better.

Harping on unhappiness or mistakes won't change a single thing. Back when I was starting a business I used to send accidental emails to the wrong people. I'd spend days harping on it, telling myself how it's so reckless of a mistake and how it was unprofessional. But here's the thing as much as I harped on it, it didn't "unsend" my email. But here's what I started to tell myself instead.

First off everyone makes mistakes and most likely people will forget about my email. But it's also free advertising for my company. There could be a chance that they will click onto my link in my email signature. Or someone might even respond back to me which opens up space for having a dialogue.

Another time I was pitching a client and accidentally sent an email to a real popular podcast asking to see if they were interested in having my client for a guest interview. That same podcast producer read my email and actually responded by suggesting I reach out to another podcast my client was more suited for. All this from a mistaken email. It just shows that mistaken emails do help advertise your company!

Speaking of tech, technology is great but use it as a tool instead of the source of your happiness. Spending time surfing Instagram, Tik Tok, and Facebook is a choice. If you're looking to be inspired to happiness on social media or any other technological means it won't happen. Matter of fact the more time you spend on social media, the more you end up being saddened by what life should be. Let me tell you between the filters, accolades, and pretty pictures social media is predominantly fabricated.

Your happiness doesn't live on social media. Someone once told me that they were depressed looking at my Instagram feed because it looked like I was doing exciting things and working on so many cool projects. Here's the truth, it's not that easy. It took a lot of sweat, blood and tears. A lot of trial and error, hundreds of no's, and thousands of dollars that went into testing. Let's not mention all these posts were only the finality of finished work that took months of hard labor, emails, phone calls, and creating opportunities from nothing. All those things, people don't tell you about on social media. We as humans are quick to show the world our accomplishments- our wins and less motivated to talk about our losses.

That's why when I landed my first TEDx Talk, *"Lonely AF: Lonely About Failure,"* I wanted to talk about our non-wins and my most intimate thoughts that I didn't tell people. Your wins do not equate to happiness. You can be a winner in every aspect of life and still be unhappy while holding onto all the excuses for your unhappiness. You can be a bazillionaire and still have excuses as to why life sucks.

The point I'm trying to make is that no matter what, happiness is something that WE CREATE. It's not something that's given to us. When was the last time you met someone who had excuses for everything and was a truly happy person? I haven't.

You're probably wondering, "how do I choose happiness?" Well, it's really simple you just do. Don't overthink it because the more you overthink your choice, the more doubts start to creep in. All you need to do is to choose and follow your happiness.

Now for those of you who don't know what will make you happy, I get it. I didn't know what made me happy for ten years. The only thing I knew in those ten years that brought me happiness was fine dining and buying expensive things. I kept asking myself what makes me happy and the answer that kept echoing back was a resounding, "I don't know!"

The one thing I did know was that being free in life always made me feel good. Free of judgments from others, free of constant worrying, free of stress, essentially I was looking for a financially abundant and peaceful life. So here's how you can find what makes you happy:

1. Try New Things

For those who are hesitant to try new things, get over it and just go for it. Get out of your comfort zone. You won't know if something new will make you cringe, cry or love it until you try it.

2. Test and Fail

It's all about trial and error, there's really no sure shot way to finding your happiness. Our happiness is completely customized towards each of us. What makes me happy might not make you happy. For example, there are people who find happiness being in a crowd and there are ones like myself that can't stand big crowds and find happiness in one on one personal experiences and sometimes solitude.

3. Read and Learn

I'm not joking about this one. Read, read, and read more. Books give you clues, people share their experiences that give you an opportunity to learn about happiness. Not a reader? No worries, listen to your books. Either way, you want to consistently learn. Learning also contributes to happiness. Most people who aren't happy aren't really learning anything new. For me, I'm obsessed with learning, it brings sheer happiness to me.

4. Never Negotiate Your Happiness

That's right your happiness is not a negotiation. Once you find it, it's your job to make sure that you have it at all times. The moment we start to chip away at what makes us happy is the moment that we fall back into the unhappiness cycle. You worked too hard to find your happiness so why would you negotiate it away that quickly?

5. Your Values Matter

We all have a set of values that we won't compromise and shouldn't. In the wake of situations that challenge your values, make sure you're holding strong. When we don't have values we lose our North Star. Our values are our personal guiding post whether it's in life or in business. Use it wisely.

If happiness means sitting around the house in your underwear so be it. Or if your happiness is building businesses, go out there and build businesses. You don't need anyone's approval, you just need to be happy doing it as long as in the process you're not hurting people on purpose.

Happiness is one thing. But being purposefully happy really changes your life! What do I mean? Once you've obtained your happiness what will you do with it? How will you change the world? In today's world where we've become dependent on tech and almost despots when it comes to our emotions, it's key to pay it forward creating happiness moments for others.

Some might argue that paying forward happiness dangerously falls into the realm of pleasing people and here's what I say to that, it's all about boundaries. You want to be able to be happy with a purpose without losing your own integrity, values, and self-worth.

If you want to build deep meaningful connections that touch the soul, it starts with emotions. How someone makes us feel we will always remember that. If we go back in time, can you remember who was your first kiss? Most of you will likely say yes, and I'll ask you why? You see if we put aside the fact that it was your first kiss, in actuality it's how the person made you feel. What about your heartbreaks? I'm sure we can all name our top three heartbreaks, why? The same reason they all evoked an emotion from us.

We can even take it out of the context of people and look at it from a brands and businesses perspective. If a brand or business gives you the feels, what will you do? You most likely will share this brand with friends and family or even post it online shouting out how amazing they are. But if a brand makes you feel bad, or provides horrible customer service, will you buy from them again? Definitely not. Will you ask for a refund of your money? The answer is "HELL YA!" Some might go as far as even writing a bad online review, telling others of their unhappy experience.

Happiness comes down to the fact that it's a commodity. A commodity that so many of us chase after, businesses survive off of, love flourishes from, and all around makes the world a better place. With so many benefits to happiness, why not choose it all the time and drop the excuses? Living and dying by happiness is a life worth living. Choose to see the joy in every situation because to every challenge there's a positive and negative side. That's just how the world works so it's up to YOU which choice you want to make.

But know that living a life of negative energies and emotions will never bring you the freedom of joy. In fact it will continue to shackle you in a non-ending cycle of depressive drab. When we reframe our excuses and change the way we look at the world miracles happen. If you're not willing to believe in the magic of life with childlike faith, then how can you expect to find happiness.

Stop lying to yourself, if you don't like when people lie to you why would you do it to yourself? Just because there's no one there to bear witness to you lying to yourself doesn't make it right. You need to set a standard for yourself even if it's painful.

Excuse hoarding just takes up room in your life that doesn't allow for new experiences or emotions to come into your world. They will NEVER buy you happiness.

LESSON 4: NO ONE OWES YOU ANYTHING

Sergio Delavicci, actor in John Wick 3 said it best, *"You leave this world the same way you came in, with nothing and empty-handed."* That right there is a real hard pill to swallow but it couldn't ring truer. We came into the world with nothing, not even clothing, so where along the way did we start to feel like the world owes us something?

If you ever need a dose of reality check and a hard lesson in humbleness, I'd suggest trying to go bankrupt and become an entrepreneur. That experience right there will humble you like a shot of Tequila and shock your system into reality. Let's be honest, no one promises us anything in the world- there's no guarantee.

Every opportunity, idea, or dream starts with YOU! Nothing and I mean nothing will happen if you're waiting on the sidelines for the right opportunity or perfect moment. No one's handing out opportunities, it's up to us to represent ourselves. We have to be our own biggest advocate, cheering ourselves on when no one is clapping for us. That's one of the hardest things to do because as humans we're built to connect, share our wins and stories.

Right now in our society when wins are all about real-time results and instant gratification, we've become conditioned to have an insatiable desire for immediate outcomes. Instant anything has become our dopamine which stems from our need to race against time. We search for hacks to get our desired results. We automize parts of our lives and consciously pass by the moments that take our breath away.

Time is so valuable and we've all come to understand how much we can possibly accomplish with just more time. That's precisely why entrepreneurs mastered the concept of outsourcing. Today most of our needs can be outsourced, from dating to vitamins and meals. I'm not saying this is a bad thing because I'm a firm believer in outsourcing anything that will not align with your goals.

But most importantly I think what many of us miss, is that once we have freed up our time by outsourcing, we need to fill it with worthwhile, meaningful projects and opportunities. These pockets of time that we've gained shouldn't be idly wasted.

We're all given finite time together this lifetime and I deeply implore you to live life with a purpose, be happy with a purpose. In college, I was very angry at the world because at a young age I experienced a tremendous amount of traumas. I ended up walking around with a chip on my shoulder. One day a friend said to me, "You know, no one owes you anything in this world, you ain't nobody." That one piece of advice made me even angrier but looking back, that was probably one of the BEST advice I've gotten. He was right no one owes a thing.

When you embrace that statement and approach life through this concept of an empty vessel you become a sponge. You're opening yourself up to all the universe to fill you with wonders and the magic of life. Twenty years after hearing that advice, I learned to just be an open vessel that's willing to be filled with experiences that bring me happiness.

We don't get to barter our time and life lessons. Meaning there are no negotiations when it comes to learning. Learning is only done through time, active participation in life, and the willingness to be open up. Instead of expecting anything just be open to receiving, I know some of you are reading this and cringing but hear me out.

Many of us are uncomfortable with graciously receiving without expectations and the same is true vice versa. Imagine for a second that you meet someone who just wants to give without anything in return. Giving to them is just joy. It is our responsibility to not just graciously receive but also reciprocate with grace.

When we're receiving, what happens? There's this emotion of gratitude and through time that gratitude towards what you were receiving might dwindle. So that's why it's important to reciprocate without expectations, that way we keep the gratitude continuously flowing between people.

Now imagine that this multiplies, these same people give and receive without expectations to ten, hundred, thousands of others then what happens? For starters, there'll probably be more happiness in the world and we would be in a perpetually productive cycle of gratitude.

It can get lonely out there so I've got you! Just because no one owes you anything, doesn't mean you're running solo. Oh, definitely not! Go out there and find a tribe of like-minded folks. If you're going to say there's no one out there, I call BS on you. I'm not here to sugarcoat things.

There are plenty of people who share the same values and beliefs as you do. Even though we're all different, we also do share some of the same basic foundations and beliefs. Whether it's race, color, religion, pet-lovers, introverts, extroverts, coffee lovers, foodies, you name it there's something there for everyone. I tell you this because it's from personal experience, I don't want you to walk the same path I did. Isolation.

My journey and obsession with building businesses had led me to spend 6 years with very few friends and definitely not a lot of people to connect with. Along the way what ends up happening is that you get really good at having conversations with yourself. Here's the fun part, if you're stuck in a situation and you have internal conversations with YOU about this, I'm pretty sure you're not going anywhere.

Why?

Easy, if you're the problem in any situation how then are you taking advice from the same person who's causing the problem? Ah-ha! This is why you need to get yourself a tribe of other people who get you but also can act as a sounding board. You can run ideas and questions past while having a support system. It doesn't mean you have to always take their advice but they might just inspire you enough to open your mind to a new perspective.

Bottom line is, find yourself a group of like-minded people. Trust me, you don't need a huge squad, I only have 4 people in my life that I confide in whether it's personal or business one of which is my dog who by the way is a total vault when it comes to secrets.

This leads me to my next point, brace yourself, it's a little cliche but I promise you there's truth in this. Teamwork makes the dreamwork. Look, as much as you want full control of every aspect of life, I'm telling you having a team is golden.

Especially when you have a team of people who have the same vision and mission as you. A team that is willing to work together to accomplish one universal goal, whatever it is, it doesn't quite matter. Just find your people!

In the process, the biggest lesson I learned was the art of letting go. It's quite difficult especially for us entrepreneurs and like any muscle, it takes daily practice. When I first started this practice of letting go it was like pulling teeth until I realized that there's something there that equates to stillness.

Many meditation masters promote being still and listening. This couldn't be more true when it comes to letting go. The reason being you end up learning about yourself and those around you. There's growth in letting go. You don't realize how powerful you are until you have to let things go. I call it an artform because everyone does *"letting go"* differently. Some of us have a full-on conversation with ourselves before we even take action. Others simply just do it without a second thought and some of us go through an entire regiment before we can do it.

There's really no right or wrong way of going about it, as long you know what and when to let go- that's the key. Our letting go threshold isn't going to be the same either. We need to use our own creative powers to attain that endpoint.

By letting go you're also making space for new experiences and people to come into your life. That is where the growing happens! I'll give you an example, have you ever seen the house of a hoarder? It's filled with so many useless things to the point where there's no space left to walk. When we hold onto things on an emotional level that's what we're doing- emotional hoarding.

For the most part, emotional hoarding isn't any different than actual hoarding of objects and it's definitely not going to promote growth. As a matter of fact, it bogs you down. This is what is known as emotional baggage.

Our emotional baggage comes in all forms from traumas to pain, all of which stem from our past experiences. As easy as it is to say, "get over it," I'm also going to tell you that it's not easy parsing through all our experiences unless we are still and willing to let go. Sometimes it even includes letting go of people who are no longer part of our personal journey and growth.

All this comes full circle as to why we need to get ourselves a tribe of like-minded folks to help us level-up and continue to grow individually and collectively.

LESSON 5: CALLING TIME OUT

Life isn't meant to be lived always on the go. There's this notion out there that it's cool to live a busy life. Have you noticed that being busy is the new cool? Newsflash it's not cool, especially when you don't allow time to recharge and really take a moment to reflect. One of the brilliant minds I highly admire is Bill Gates. Even as one of the world's notable billionaires he too takes time outs. He calls those, "Think Weeks."

I think it's a brilliant idea, to take time out to think with no distractions. Gates uses that week to read, think about world problems and how he can come up with solutions to make the world a better place.

Today we're so glued to our phones and our validity is based on what others think of us. The constant dopamine hit that we get from checking our Instagram posts doesn't really help create mind blowing changes in the world. It's definitely not helping us better connect with each other if we're busy participating in the heads down culture.

There was a time that I didn't have social media and to this day I don't own a TV or watch the news. Back in the day when I was growing up there wasn't any social media or cellphones matter of fact communication was done mostly through postal mail. It's something about the wait of getting a response back from the other person. That small act was an exercise in patience and desire. Today we communicate with emojis that represent what we're trying to say. I know I sound like a dinosaur but I digress.

When we spend our time on the go and working, we leave little time to ourselves. Someone else always seems to need us, our bosses, spouses, employees, kids, even pets. I think it's time that we start calling timeouts.

There's nothing wrong with taking time for yourself to recharge and recalibrate. It not only helps you get present, it also creates a better version of you for those you love. Part of my time out is a total tech detox where I put the phone on airplane mode or shut it off completely. No communication in or out. During this time I use it to focus on building my businesses, researching things I'm curious about, figuring out solutions to my clients' problems, writing, or taking power naps. I always joke with people that they really shouldn't use me as their emergency contact because it'll be hard to get a hold of me.

Aside from the phone detox, my phone doesn't ring, ding, or vibrate. So anytime there's an incoming I usually end up missing it. If someone needed to really get a hold of me they would have to email me. I've been asked many times in interviews, "how exactly do you even run a business if your phone is always silent." My response is that I've had my phone silent for the last eighteen years of my life and managed to build five companies during that time.

I remembered that one time I had an ex say to me, "why is it that your phone is always off? That seems so shady." Shady or not my sanity and mental well-being comes first and this is part of what it takes for me to be in my element.

My point is this calling time out can come in many different forms but the important takeaway is that your time out has to work for you. It needs to be something that you can easily build into your life. You don't need to spend a million dollars to have a time out. It can be small things such as turning off your phone.

This is a crucial step to our self-care. Too often we get self-care confused with doing materialistic things like vacations and visits to the salon. Yes that can be part of self-care and timeouts but there's something much bigger when you take the time to purposefully grow and learn as a person.

I've gotten this far in life because I've taken the time to have reflective moments that allow me to grow as a person. I guess it also helps as I'm a severe introvert which means I need the alone time to recharge. I know you wouldn't have guessed that I'm an introvert.

***

Now why do I call timeouts a lesson? Well we're in a societal time warp that condones busy. At work we have meetings about meetings and multi-tasking seems to be some sort of trophy. It's definitely something that we have gotten wrong. We're no longer stopping to take in a moment and enjoy it. Breathe it in, dwell on it a little because once this moment passes we won't get another one like it.

I truly believe that life is made up of moments and experiences, good and bad. If we just take that time to relish in the moment we would probably have better lives. Some of you might be asking, "well what about the bad moments, do you mean relish in those too?" Yes I do! I'm not saying to dwell on them and relive it like you're watching a movie in slow motion. It's about taking in the bad moments, acknowledging it and then letting it go.

What's the use of doing this? Anything bad that happens to us we need to grieve it. Think about when we break up with someone. Some of us cry it out and then hop onto the next rebound relationship. We never really heal that hurt but instead we end of carrying the hurt into the next relationship and the next till it becomes a vicious cycle. Then one day we're left wondering why are we so angry and bitter?

That's the same that happens when we don't take a timeout to relish in the bad moments, learn from it and find solutions to make it better the next time around. We're too quick to accept that being stuck in the same bad mistake is ok and that it's always someone else's fault. How about you didn't do the work so it keeps coming back to you?

Take in the bad moments. It's ok. But also relish in the great moments. Those are the moments that take your breath away, that touch the human spirit and make you cry. I'm the first one to admit to you that I'm a crier. Don't let the tough exterior fool you, I cry often and I'm not ashamed to say it because crying for me is a release and reminder that I'm still human. I haven't allowed the outside world to harden me. It also means that I'm alive but still have an opportunity to be better.

When I was growing up I was told to work hard in life and I watched my parents work extremely hard to build a life for us. But what I also learned was that they never stopped to consciously build their marriage and work on themselves as individuals. Eventually both my parents were just surviving in a world of chasing money to support our lifestyle. My father ended up drinking too much and my mother worked multiple jobs.

As an adult I vowed to never live like that, instead I want to experience things and moments that leave me in awe and touch my heart in ways that words can't explain. Don't get me wrong, I work hard but I also am very conscious in knowing what it is I want to feel from life.

PART 2: DREAM LIKE NO ONE'S LOOKING

Don't whisper your dreams to the universe, shout it out!

This is probably one of my favorite past times that I can't live without. Inside my mind, there's a whole world that I love living in, most of the time at least. I know I sound crazy but like I said I'm keeping it very real for you. The beauty of us humans is our capacity to dream. We dare to imagine the impossible, the things that change lives and magical moments that bring joy to each one of us on a very personal level.

It's those who are crazy enough to dream big and think they can change the world who actually do. Can you believe that? All this just from the simple act of dreaming, which by the way is FREE, it costs nothing to dream. So I challenge you to dream big, bigger than you can ever imagine.

Our dreams, just seeing those words on my screen as I write this book gives me googly eyes because it feels like limitless freedom. Dreams are our minds' playground. Here's the truth no matter what, don't let anyone shatter your dreams. I can't tell you how many times family members have tried to shatter my dreams from as early on as my childhood.

I remember in the second grade I wanted to be an author and my mom said to me, "You don't get good grades in reading and writing. How will you be a writer? You can forget about that." So I changed my mind and said, "I wanted to be a fashion designer." Again I was shot down when I was told, "you're not even good at drawing." To all you dreamers out there, I DARE YOU TO DREAM.

DREAM 1: BELIEVING IN YOU

The beginning of any dream requires YOU to believe in yourself, even when people tell you, you're crazy.

I've heard it so many times, "You're crazy for having your own business," and if I gave up each time I heard those words, I wouldn't have the stories, battle scars, and expertise to share with the world. Let me tell you while I was miserably working in corporate, deep down I wanted to own my own business. The thought of being able to dictate my own terms, work on projects that excite me, and have the freedom to do what I want to do was and still is my WHY. But I was too scared to take the crazy leap.

It took me six years to draw up the courage to even start taking steps in the direction of my dreams. During those sixteen years of working for someone else's dreams, I got fired from corporate jobs five times.

My entrepreneurial journey is far from pretty. I have the scars to prove it because I have three failed businesses, founded five companies, co-founded one company, lost every dollar to my name, lost my Manhattan apartment and it took five years to land my first TEDx Talk.

All this because I knew that there was no way I was going back to corporate. The thought of working with a sales quota and having meetings about meetings was enough for me to make entrepreneurship work. Not to mention the office politics and the idle chit chats about shopping and sitcoms that made me want to barf.

The first company I started was a life coaching business because it was "trending." I quickly learned that there's no way I can handle listening to people's problems 24/7. So I quickly shut that business down. When it came to my second business I thought to myself ok, "Connie, what are you good at?" I figured since I spent most of my career in luxury that I was going to start a luxury concierge business. Now, mind you I really didn't have a clue what luxury concierges really did other than get people "stuff." As you guessed that business didn't even get off the ground.

At this point, I'm thinking to myself, "I need a come to JESUS moment because I'm out of ideas for another business." I asked myself, "Ok what else are you good at?" The answer, I went to college and got a marketing degree. Just like that, I opened up a marketing agency geared towards yoga studios.

That was the wrong move. If you know anything about yoga studios it's this, they generate small amounts of revenue. Now unless the studios are backed by a large corporate company there's really no extra money for these businesses to outsource marketing efforts. You guessed it, this business got shut down too. But the good news is that out of all this my current company was born, an award-winning public relations and brand management agency, The Chi Group.

I tell you all this because I want you all to know that I didn't just wake up one day and have a business idea that worked. I had to first believe in myself, believe that I was able to do this and believe that I would find a business idea that would feel right for me. Too often we put this added pressure on ourselves to "know" exactly what kind of business we're going to start.

When in fact being an entrepreneur is really about testing, retesting, failing and testing some more. Every time an idea didn't work I didn't get too upset because I'd always tell myself this is simply play time- a curiosity experiment. If you shift the way you approach new ideas and concepts you take away the pressure of must-knowing the answer to everything.

I want you to get over yourself and stop operating on the notion that you have to have it all figured out. Heck, even today I'll admit it I don't have it all figured out sometimes I'm learning on the fly when I'm presented with new challenges. No matter what the challenge you MUST believe in yourself first. If you don't believe in you, how can you expect others to believe in you?

It's funny because on my entrepreneur journey my mom once said to me, "why don't you give up already. You keep testing and trying with no big results." I had to laugh because what she didn't know was that the personal gains outweighed the big wins for me. She would nag me about going back to corporate or getting a part-time job at Target. As you can imagine at this point I was tired of her nagging.

I haven't polished up a resume in who knows how long. Not to mention I'm pretty sure I'm not exactly employee material. I had to make a point to my mom. I actually updated my resume and for the section of most recent employment I wrote in there entrepreneur for the last six years. To this day I still remember putting together that resume because it made my skin itch.

I then sent out thirty resumes online from part-time to full-time jobs across various industries and waited. No one called me back or emailed me to offer me a position. One company even flat out told me I'm overqualified. Of course, I had to gloat and tell mom the results of this little experiment.

The other reason why it's hard to give up our businesses as entrepreneurs is for the simple fact that our identity is entwined into all our business. If today you take away the business from most entrepreneurs they're left with the question, "who am I?" I've been through so many moments where I felt like closing the business. But the panic sets in once I start to contemplate, well what do I do now? Who am I without my business?

That's why you have to believe in who you are, your passions, and dreams. No one and I mean no one can stop you. One of my life-long dreams was to meet Sir Richard Branson, whom I really admire not just for his marketing chops but also for his philanthropic work. That dream finally came true when a couple of years ago I found out that he was going to speak in NYC.

My meeting with Branson is something I will never forget and will probably tell this story to my grandchildren because not only was it a dream come true for me but I managed to embarrass myself in the process.

After Branson gave a riveting interview, it was time for Q&A's. Before the event, I promised myself that I would be brave enough to get up and ask him a question. But when I saw the double lines of 20+ people deep, I gave up. Instead I waited for him to come out the stage door and autograph the book I had just purchased. As he rushed towards his car I tailed alongside him and was ready to ask my well rehearsed question pertaining to marketing. Instead what came rolling out my mouth was this, "Richard will you mentor me?"

I was completely mortified that I just asked the world's highly respected entrepreneur who just so happens to run billion dollar companies to mentor me! At this point I couldn't take it back other than walk alongside him waiting for his answer. Branson being Branson, replied with his cool British accent, "I'm sorry I'm not able to." Funny thing was, I wasn't even crushed about it at all.

Instead as Richard got into his car and fans were being pushed back by security, I quickly whipped out my business card and while the car door was closing, I flung my business card into his lap. I watched this happen in slow motion like a scene out of the Matrix when Neo dodged all the bullets.

Now here's the deal, I knew for a fact that Branson has my information. I saw it go into his lap. The next day I checked the backend of my website and saw there was a visit from somewhere in the UK. It's been five years and I'm still waiting to see if Branson will mentor me.

Another entrepreneur that I also admire was Daymond John, one of the founders of Fubu also known as one of the Sharks on the show, "Shark Tank." I knew that I wanted to meet him and really get a chance to understand how he thinks. It was through the power of social media that I found a way.

It was publicized that Daymond was going to be in NYC to launch a new collection of his fashion line. Since I am the owner of a PR agency and also a contributor writer for various blogs, I was able to get into the event. What was amazing was that I had a chance to meet Daymond and sit down with him. As he imparted his wisdom I remembered having my groupie moment and thought to myself, "Oh my GOD I'm really sitting next to one of the most admired entrepreneurs in the world and he's actually talking to ME!"

The man graciously gave me 15 minutes of his time. In the entrepreneur world 15 minutes is a BIG deal because in 15 minutes we can accomplish so many things. Now if today I didn't believe that I would one day meet some of the world's leading minds in business I probably wouldn't have met any of them.

Believing in yourself is the first step to accomplishing your dreams. Do you know how many times people didn't believe in me? Too many to count. This is also true when I started speaking on stages. I promise you there wasn't a line of people that believed in me, matter of fact, no one did. Until I came across a woman who was in charge of finding speakers for events. She took a chance on me, believed in me the way I believed in myself and booked me onto a stage at the Javits Center in NYC.

It only takes one person to change the trajectory of your life, take a chance on you. But the biggest thing is YOU HAVE TO believe in you! It's a must. You might not know the exact steps to getting your desired outcomes but when we have blind faith something happens. I don't know if you notice it but I do. It seems like the universe or GOD just somehow shifts everything to align for you. Believing is just the beginning of the magic, you still have to put in the work to make it into a reality.

DREAM 2: ONE DAY SYNDROME

One day I'm going to... STOP right there- no you're not. If you're starting a sentence with one day, most likely you won't do it. The one-day syndrome is exactly that one day I will fill in the blank. Too often many of us have dreams of one day we will but if we're not taking immediate actions for our dreams, the fire dies. Every day you say one day it will be a day that your dreams are dying.

It's great to dream but you also have to take daily steps towards that dream. We have to set standards and goals to achieve what most might think is impossible. Now it doesn't mean that you'll be successful on the first try but if you're willing to keep going eventually those dreams will become a reality. Whatever action you take it doesn't have to be some gigantic newsworthy action, it can be something small.

Let's say you want to eat better, it doesn't mean that tomorrow you throw out all the junk food in your cabinets. You start slow. Many years ago I transitioned from being a meat-eater to full-on vegetarian. I didn't do it overnight but I did take baby steps learning from someone who had Crohn's disease on how he transitioned his diet.

He taught us to start small, instead of eating meat seven days a week do five days of meat and two days of fish. Then slowly increase the days you eat fish to seven days. From there, five days fish two days veggies until you become seven days veggies. It's easier to build a whole new diet that way.

That's the same mindset you need to implement when it comes to making your dreams happen. The small steps determine your successes. There'll be days you fall off the wagon, but remember to give yourself grace-just get right back on and start over.

My one-day syndrome turned into a sixteen-year stint of working for someone else. Do I regret it? No, not at all because it afforded me the luxury of gaining skills that I would've otherwise not learned. Do I wish I learned the lesson earlier when it comes to taking action while the fire's hot? You bet and that's why when an idea comes to mind nowadays, I make it a habit to take action as quickly as possible. It doesn't matter what steps I take as long as I'm moving forward.

The other infamous statement that goes hand in hand with the one-day syndrome is, "I don't have time." This one right here- is the most dangerous statement because it's like the gateway drug to procrastination. We all have the same amount of time now what we do with it is completely up to us.

I'm not saying that you have to operate a life of constant on the go, that's not healthy either. In fact, what I'm saying is that life is about a balance of finding the time and spending time in the right places. You need to figure out what are your priorities and where you're going to place your efforts. Let's say you want to start a business but you spend all your time reading comics when time passes and you realize it's been a year of no progress then who's fault is it?

You have to take responsibility for your time. Some people are so stringent that they log every minute what they spend time on and how much time they use. I'm definitely not that militant about it but I am very picky where and who I afford my time to. That's the precise reason why a couple of years ago I made a hardline decision to stop taking coffee meetings.

Yes, I know you read all these blogs that say take coffee meetings that's how business is done. I'm going to disagree. Based on my personal experiences what I noticed was that during these coffee meetings, no business really comes out of it. Matter of fact it's more of a brain-picking session by the other person and after it's done I feel like I had the energy sucked out of me.

On top of that, I did a calculation of how much it was costing me to go on these coffee meetings and the result was a whopping $1,560 USD if I took three coffee meetings a week for a whole year. To be honest, that's $1,560 I could invest back into my business or into my own personal growth and learning.

Time to me is the MOST precious commodity that I own and every minute that I'm not doing something for the betterment of self, my business or helping others who want to be helped is a minute wasted. Sometimes you need to learn to say no to opportunities especially if it's going to take more time out of your schedule and learn to outsource.

I want you to be mindful of your time, be careful with it and yes be picky what you put your time and energy towards. The more time and energy we spend on things the more love and emotional attachment we have to it. Definitely keep that top of mind as you go about chasing your wildest dreams. Diligently do time inventory and make sure you're time allocation aligns with your dreams.

One day in the distant future you want to be able to look your dreams in the eye and say that you gave it the best time of your life. Time never waits for any of us and it will continue to go on with or without us.

DREAM 3: OUR BAD DREAMS

Bad dreams, bad dreams go away, good dreams good dreams are here to stay... But will you let it? We all dream of dreams, some are big, some small, while other dreams we don't dare share with the world. But in reality, we all have bad dreams. Those dreams that stop us dead in our tracks and paralyze us from taking action. That's called OUR FEARS. Yes we all have them and some of us are ruled by our fears. Unfortunately, that'll be the quickest way we lose grip of reality.

You see the thing with fear is that it basically breaks down to false expectations appearing real. Most of the time the things that we fear never come true while other times our fears have a funny way of playing itself out in real-time. So what do you fear?

Is it the fear of failure or maybe the fear of success? Maybe this might fit better, the fear of being broke, perhaps the fear of never being enough, not lovable, the list of our bad dreams goes on forever. But will you let that stop you from really living the life that YOU deserve? A life filled with the freedom to dream and create your reality on a scope that is unimaginable.

We battle our fears every day and here's the truth, no one is coming to save you. There's no superhero that'll come swooping in to magically eradicate your fears. So if you're waiting for someone to do just that, let me save you time and tell you it's not happening. Well, if no one's coming to save us then what?

It's up to you to study your fears, understand why you have this fear. That's the first step to healing it? Fear can sometimes be a great thing, it can save your life. But like anything in life, it needs to be a balance. What messages were you taught when it comes to your fears?

For the longest time, I battled the fear of success. It's a pretty common one for a lot of entrepreneurs because with great success comes great responsibilities. I worried that I couldn't live up to those fabricated expectations of what an entrepreneur is supposed to look like. Especially what was demonstrated in the world. You see I didn't really have an entrepreneur role model that was beside me when I was creating my businesses.

All I've learned is first-hand knowledge that came with a lot of trying and falling. Some of the lessons I learned were very hard. In my mind to become a successful entrepreneur you were supposed to be like a Richard Branson. Yes in many ways that is true but I didn't know if I could live up to that kind of success metric. I mean come on, it's Richard Branson. He's a marketing genius, philanthropist and had attempted to settle disputes between leaders of rival countries.

That's a big responsibility because one person has the potential to change the lives of so many people without anyone really knowing it. I thought about this many nights and asked myself if I'd be able to do that? Would I have the mental and emotional capacity and wisdom to really move a nation on that level? The honest answer is not yet. But the fear was still there, it was that voice in the back of my head that would creep up every time I had successfully accomplished something.

The funny thing is that today many people tell me that I'm successful. To me, I really don't feel that way because I'm simply living my dreams. Here's how I flipped the meaning of success on its head. I created a definition, one that felt right for me. Success to me is having the courage to chase your dreams and make it a reality.

Why does this work because I completely removed the pressure of living up to an ideal. A standard that in my mind that seems almost unreachable. It took me years to come up with this idea. But simply reframing the concept of success I've now been able to align it with my life without stressing myself out. So the question becomes do you need success to be happy or do you need happiness to be successful?

Along the way, the fear of success wasn't my only fear. Growing up I was plagued with fears inherited from a generational cycle of lack thereof. I also battled the fear of not having money, that's a biggie for me and the reason why I work so hard. I watched my parents struggle for money as a kid and it definitely imprinted its genetic makeup onto me.

The only way I knew how to placate that fear was to work for someone else's dreams, getting a paycheck every two weeks. But I was miserably unhappy. When I started my business my biggest fear came true.

I was used to making close to six figures then suddenly one day there's zero in your bank account. It's the most harrowing feeling ever. I don't think I can even start to describe it in words, other than distress. As if it wasn't bad enough not having a dollar to my name, I lost my Manhattan apartment. The amount of pain you feel when this happens is really mind-blowing.

For most of my life I was taught to have money, make money, save money and then one-day the lesson that was drilled into me all of a sudden gets disproved now what I do? This was the moment that I needed to look my biggest fear in the face, take a deep breath and here's what I told myself, "You made it once, you'll make it again. But this time on your terms." So I experienced broke on every single spectrum possible because I wanted to understand my fear behind not having money.

Not having money is part of the journey but staying broke is a personal choice. It's ok to not have the money when you're embarking on a new journey. Here's what I learned about not having money, you get scrappy and super creative. Not just that you make things work. It's definitely a lesson that even still today has shaped a lot of how I live. I call it "creative living." Having no money is definitely not a fun experience. But it is one of the biggest lessons you'll encounter in life. If you take a look at many entrepreneurs they have a similar story of being broke or homeless. Mark Cuban perfect example, at one point he was living out of his car and eating ketchup sandwiches to survive.

I also dealt with the fear of not being enough, oh was this a big one too! As a kid, my mom often compared me to other kids who were doing better than I was. By the way, this is an essential part of Asian "Tiger Mom" parenting. It was a cultural thing amongst many Asian families. I truly believe that this type of parenting may have contributed to birthing a generation of Asian kids who are afraid to speak up for what they believe in. Instead, these same kids would work extremely hard to overcompensate and be better than others whether it was in school, in their career, life, etc.

Imagine having this message drilled into you day in and day out. What ends up happening is that you lose sight of the barometric level of what is enough. There's no real endpoint, so what happens is that you keep struggling in a direction of life that's essentially someone else's quota of what "success" looks like. The end result is straight up unhappiness.

When I realized all this and connected the dots I finally understood that happiness, success, and knowing you are enough actually all go hand in hand, it was a light bulb moment for me. EUREKA! Now the next question is how do you undo decades of malware and rewire your own brain? The answer, piece by piece. There's no shortcut, no app, no filter, none of that. It's putting in the work on a daily basis and catching yourself when you speak ill of yourself whether in your head or out loud.

Our bad dreams will always have a way of creeping up on us, but it's our own responsibility to quell the monsters-slay the dragons. If we don't they will keep coming back to us over and over again. So be gentle with your fears yet bold enough to face them. It won't always be fun and it definitely won't always feel great. But once we've conquered our biggest fears we end up feeling better in the long run.

I'm not perfect because even till this day my bad dreams creep up on me and I find myself reminding myself that I went through hell and back. I survived it all. Maybe I have a few bruises here and there but I proudly display my battle scars.

DREAM 4: DO IT FOR THE LOVE

To love and be loved this lifetime is the most precious gift. We all want love. I don't care if you're an alpha burly guy, a nerdy introvert woman, a sweet child, or some cute cuddly four-legged furbaby, we all need it. Love comes in so many forms.

For some, it's the search for a loving, caring, supportive, encouraging endearing, best friend, soulmate, and life partner. For others, it's about finding love with someone who they can build trust, loyalty while having that chemistry. There's a love between parent and child and the most infamous love of ages, Romeo and Juliet (one of my favorites). There's the love of food, love of babies, cute things, etc. But no matter how you define love it's the basis of why we exist.

When we have the ability to love and receive love something magical happens to us. Not only does it change our bodies' chemistry but love changes our emotional well-being. For me, love is intricate, complex, and beautiful because it's an art form. It's also the space where you stretch your limits, find yourself and lose yourself. It's in the tough times, the moments that make you laugh and cry that you learn the strength of love and the capacity in which the human spirit can stretch in the name of love.

For so many of us, we're quick to love someone else but neglect to love ourselves as a daily practice. Loving ourselves isn't about buying things, making tons of money or taking a few yoga classes. Today we've watered down the definition of self-love. It's become commercialized and commoditized instead self-love is about caring for our mental well-being. It's more important today because we're in a world that over stimulates so many of our senses. We're at a time where hearts and thumbs up set the tone for self-worth. It's no longer about a practice of growing and being curious. Loving yourself is all about investing in yourself and not about someone else validating you.

Depending on others to give you love can lead to disappointments and let downs. In my 20's I constantly looked outside of myself for love whether it was in the form of relationships, buying expensive handbags, fine dining, etc. I looked everywhere and never within. What ended up happening was I was heartbroken to the point that I lost myself.

I spent my teens, 20's and even my early 30's in a lot of painful situations. I was crying from the inside out and didn't even know that I was the one who I needed to love first. In fact, it's all about healing from our past experiences.

Currently, I no longer search for love outside of myself because I've come to realize that the love I have for me is enough. The funny thing was when I was preparing for my first TEDx Talk about entrepreneurship and how it's a lonely road I got curious as to whether or not we could quantify love. More so I used dating because that's the precipice to finding love. We go on dates to determine if someone is appropriate for us or if we want to further spend time with this person, which in some cases leads to love.

Here's how that looked like, I broke it down using dollars and hours. Let's say you're a consultant who runs your own business and say you charge about $200/hr. Now since you have a busy lifestyle let's also assume that you get in at least a three-dates per week minimum. Using a rough estimate of how much time is usually spent on each date plus travel time I came up with five hours.

So if we do the math, $200/hr x (5 hours x 3 dates per week) = $3,000 USD and now let's scale it and see what it looks like in a month, $12,000 and if we're consistent we do this for a year, $144,000 (*that's all USD by the way*). Now I don't know about you, but for me, that's a lot of money to spend on something with no guarantees and not to mention you can't report it as a loss on income taxes *(Disclaimer: I'm not an accountant so any tax-related questions or concerns please do consult your accountant or tax preparer)*

In other words, what I'm trying to say is there are no guarantees when it comes to depending on someone else to give you love. YOU have to be the one who provides it to yourself first.

Though I broke it down for you in numbers, the bigger thing to consider is that you're actually expounding energy on something that requires you to fill your cup first before you can pour into someone else's. If your cup has nothing in it then you're essentially able to give to the other person... Nothing.

Pouring into your own cup can be in the form of getting your spirituality right, reading books to nourish your mind, taking classes, learning about things that interest you, training your body to operate at optimal levels, or anything that doesn't require you to spend time glued to a screen scrolling through people's make-believe feeds of filters and edits.

I want nothing more for you than to dream of the love that you want and deserve. Imagine how it makes you feel. How is that love being demonstrated? Whatever results come up for you, give that to yourself 10x. If being loved means that you're hugged every day then everyday you hug yourself, mentally or actually physically doing it. I know it sounds ridiculous but I'm telling you over time it'll make a difference.

The challenge arises when we start doing things not for love but for survival. Day in and day out we're doing something that's meaningless, that doesn't feed our soul and eventually, we get so far away from what makes us feel loved. There may come a time that you fall out of love with what you used to love and that's ok too. Know that it's absolutely fine that you are entitled to shift your emotions and energies, it doesn't make you any less amazing.

It just means that you're growing, morphing and finding your way around life. You're just doing life! For me, I love entrepreneurship, the creative process of creating a business from idea to actualization. There have been many times that I stopped to ask myself am I in love with this? If tomorrow I wasn't doing this then what would I do? Whenever I think about those questions, I can't picture myself doing anything else other than building businesses and creating opportunities.

Doing it for the love doesn't always mean that it'll be smooth sailing nor does it mean that someone will just hand you the keys to the kingdom. Nope! It requires sweat equity, hard work and tons of learning for you to realize what else you love and don't. Same thing as in a relationship, you can love someone but in order to make the relationship work both sides need to put in the effort, time, and patience to grow the relationship.

Whatever you love doing I want you to keep doing it, be patient with it and be the BEST at it. Eventually, success will hit. It's an inevitable fact. But if you're only doing something to become successful I guarantee that you might not be happy doing it.

So go on and keep doing it for the love.

DREAM 5: LET'S GET WILD OR MAYBE NOT

Do you ever dream of letting loose throwing all your responsibilities away without a care in the world? Or maybe you dream of one day you'll live a little more once the kids are older or when you make more money? Oh I feel you. So I ask, are you ready to get wild?

Some of you are probably already panicking and others might be already cheering like it's 1999. Whatever your response is to that statement, don't worry I'm not going to suggest you go out and get reckless stupid. All I'm saying is I want you to take a look within and ask if you're really living life to the fullest? Are you truly being a free spirit?

I know it's tough letting go of things and even our old way of life. I've been there and sometimes catch myself going backwards. Many of us dream that we wish we could be more free in thoughts, emotions, and everything in between. I'm here to tell you it's SO do-able.

Don't wait another second decide to let go of things. You know the longer you hold onto old thoughts and emotions that don't serve you the harder it is for you to let go. I used to hold onto things all the time to the point where I was just straight angry everyday. Can you imagine living like that? It took the doctor telling me that you're starting to develop an ulcer that I started to change my ways.

How did I do it? I talked to myself ALL the time. It sounds crazy but I have internal dialogues with myself and in the beginning I was wondering if I was somehow "crazy" for talking to myself. Obviously I didn't dare utter my intimate thoughts publicly but it took many meetings with myself for me to realize that holding onto shit was not making me feel better. I was missing out on so many happy moments that created more meaning. On top of that I was spending time focusing on a lot of negative stuff.

***

The free will of choice between getting wild and staying in the shadows is also reflective of our wants and needs. These are two different things, as wants are our desires, our hopes and dreams. Needs are a must haves, non-negotiables. When we clearly learn the difference between the two we are beginning to live life on the wild side. Many people want for things, for people and outside sources to attain a life that's full. When our inside world is filled with happiness we don't want for much.

I remember the time that a dear friend of mine talked to me about making my needs clear when it comes to relationships. Though theoretically it made sense and sounded great but when put into practice I had a difficult time discerning between the both. My own language was even confusing. What were my needs, I was stating them as my wants. This clearly was incongruent and when I looked within I realized this, I was replacing the word "need" with "want" because I was afraid of being disappointed.

You see when we need something and the need isn't met it's disappointing. When we use want it lightens the load and lessens the pressure. But the downside is that you will never be fully satisfied, not having your needs met. For me I spent so much time being disappointed that I sure as hell wasn't going to consciously set myself up for anymore disappointments. Unfortunately this kind of strategy calls upon grave turbulence.

I encourage you to let loose, get wild and discover what your needs and wants are. What are your non-negotiables and have the audacity to get clear about what you need in life. Along the journey of discovery, being a free spirit allows your entire being to wander and imagine the endless possibilities of what it's really like to be free.

PART 3: DIRTY SECRETS OF OVERACHIEVERS

The deepest oceans can only keep so many secrets. What is it about secrets that we're so obsessed with it? The secret lives of celebrity gossip columns to our own secrets and even business secrets seem to take center stage in our lives. The answer- secrets is a way for us to delve into the innermost workings of people's lives and get an honest glimpse of who they are. It's also the parts that can be shameful, painful, and not so pretty. But nonetheless, it's still the TRUTH.

It's when we unearth the secrets to reveal the truth that we grow in ways that inspire and aspire, not just ourselves but those around us. By inviting you into the dirty secrets of overachievers it's my own truth that took decades of trial and error, experimenting with what seemed like great solutions to solve my personal mysteries of what life is. Though the solutions seem simple, the journey along the way was undoubtedly a dizzying maze.

Even today in full transparency I still get lost on this journey, it's a daily battle of quieting senseless brain chatter and having the courage to put one foot in front of the other. Ultimately the goal is to keep moving forward. Staying in place will only prolong your growth and selfishly you're not sharing the best version of yourself with the world. Look we all have our own version of dirty secrets. But I bet some of your secrets we might have the same one's too! By sharing my secrets with you I'd like to invite you to have the courage to share yours with the world.

SECRET 1: HELL NO AF

Oh no, say it's not so. Yep, the most magical word spelled with two little letters N-O! It's no secret that many of us struggle with saying no. In fact, I was taught that the word no meant conflict, that you're creating waves and problems. I harbored this secret for so long that I didn't understand the value of no.

In fact, many of us attach saying no to some sort of self-affirming statement such as, "if I say no it means I'm a horrible parent," or "if I say no then people won't like me." It wasn't until I became an entrepreneur that I realized how beautiful no is and it makes me wonder why I didn't use this word more often in my vocabulary.

As an entrepreneur you come in contact with people from all walks of life. But here's the truth, many people view business owners simply as a cash register. They want your business because they want to increase their sales. Take a guess as to what happens because of this mentality?

I was subjected to this and have gotten better at being a gatekeeper to my own life. Many years ago I said YES to just about every business opportunity that came streaming into my inbox and a

HELL YES to every "coffee meeting" invite. This went on for some time when I realized, wait a second I'm saying YES to all these opportunities but what am I getting in return?

My inbox became flooded with literally every company reaching out to me to entice me to buy their product before time runs out. Not only was this frustrating but it didn't make me feel valued. I was just another number on their prospect list.

Today I will be the first one to tell you that no is utilized in my vernacular so often that only really amazing business opportunities are flowing through my inbox. It's so refreshing to be able to feel organized and make forward strides when we start to implement no.

I think no gets a bad wrap sometimes and we forget that it's the gatekeeper to our sacred space and sanity. It also allows us to make space for more things that bring us joy and happiness. Now if you're wondering how to start implementing the no strategy, it's super easy. Start by responding with no thank you to an opportunity that doesn't resonate with you whether it's in person or in an email. That's it.

As we grow and enrich our lives with experiences that change us our no's will also morph and reconfigure itself in different instances. The perfect example is as a kid you might have said not to veggies and as an adult you're saying no to blind dates. However, what you say no to will also morph, don't judge it because at that moment that is what you need. Our needs will also change based on the season of life we are in.

Sometimes our no's don't necessarily need to be spoken or verbalized. It can be shown through our actions. I'm a firm believer that action speaks volumes. I'm realistic so I know that not every instance in our lives requires a verbal hard no.

People's opinions of you is a great example. We all have opinions, some great others have you scratching your head silently asking yourself WTH? When others form opinions about you, you don't have to listen to it. You don't need to internalize it either, simply learn to tune out the voices that don't matter. Entrepreneurs are great at this!

Almost every entrepreneur you talk to will tell you that people in their lives have formed some sort of negative opinion about what they're doing. The result, entrepreneurs have this uncanny way of breaking the mold and powering forward to accomplish their dreams. It's through their actions of pushing through that they are inadvertently saying, "no, your opinion doesn't matter to me."

Other times the painful fact is that you will have to say no to family and people you love. It will pain you. At the same time it shows that you are setting clear boundaries of what you will and will not tolerate. We are solely responsible for keeping guard as to what opportunities and people we allow to set foot into our space. I can not stress enough how important this is.

Too often we allow ourselves to get carried away and let people into our lives who turn around and wreak havoc. The lessons we learn from these experiences are so valuable and will definitely alter the way you conduct your life and business.

No is also a way for us to reaffirm our values. There will be instances in life and even business where you will need to say no because it doesn't align with your values. You will be tested. For example, if there is a deal on the table worth millions of dollars but it requires you to do things that don't fit your value system and beliefs. Do you take the deal or not? Well know that it's okay to give yourself permission to say no to that deal. I know you're probably thinking, "but it's millions of dollars."

That may be true but think about the consequences of saying yes to an opportunity that isn't a fit and forcing yourself to go through with it because it's a contract. As a result you might resent the opportunity or subconsciously mess it up or maybe regret even taking the deal.

On the other hand, no is a fantastic confidence builder. The more times you say "No," there's some sort of power that starts to surge through you. You almost feel like a superwoman or even superman. The reason for that is that it gives you the ability to control situations and outcomes.

***

In this world we all want to feel valued, seen, and heard. When we're saying no it's a way for us to stand and be recognized. Some might argue that you're being recognized as a rebel while others will hail you a hero. In either instance, we are seen in ways that can't be denied. So why do we want to be valued? I wonder if being valued is a way to feed our primitive egos?

Actually it goes deeper than our egos, it touches upon our basic human need for connection, to be part of something that is greater than us. Our value system is fragilely built upon our life experiences and our childhood. Bad experiences when left tethered in the wind can lapse into a lifetime echo of habits. While great experiences depending on the depth of the experience can satiate our need for connection. It can also have a lasting impact on how we connect with others. If we will be open or closed off to these experiences. These same experiences also have the potential to deepen our sense of meaning.

If we sum it all up, our need for connection and to be valued comes down to simply wanting to be loved.

SECRET 2: VULNERABILITY IS POWER

Let's get emo! It sounds scary but let's do this. Vulnerability seems to be one of those words that we throw around often but might not have the courage to practice. Some might even wonder what exactly does vulnerability even look like? Let alone put it into practice. So here's the cliff notes version on vulnerability, exposing yourself. Gasp! Why would we even think to do that? Right! I'm with you.

But you see when we keep things all bottled up and it starts to build on top of itself and what ends up happening is that you start to lose our ability to truly grow. Not to mention it also causes us to get sick and feel horrible.

True vulnerability let's us develop deep impactful relationships and strengthens our bonds with other people. The whole concept of life hinges on the relationships we build which in turn translates into the experiences we experience. We will always remember how people treat us and what feelings they conjure up within us.

Emotions are a universal language, if you think about it we can go anywhere in the world and if we see a smile, we know that person is friendly or happy. We see someone crying, we automatically know that they are in pain or sad. So why bring up emotions?

Well, emotions and vulnerability go hand in hand. We need to invest some sort of emotion in order to have the ability to be vulnerable. When we share stories, which by the way every culture and generation in the world thrives off stories because that's how we learn best. It's a way of being vulnerable. Every story has emotions that most of us can identify with.

Think of this, what makes a good story? It's a story that you want to keep listening to over and over again? It's the emotions that it evokes in you. The beauty of stories is that you and I can read the same words but we both might learn something different from the same story or even feel completely opposite emotions from each other.

When we are vulnerable with our relationships whether it's in love or business we're essentially telling a story to someone else. We're trusting that they will be non-judgmental, keepers of our secrets, or even the wise sage that will guide us past hurdles. It's also the way we allow others to understand us and get to know the deepest inner workings of how we operate.

Each one of us is uniquely complex and how we create deep and meaningful relationships comes down to one thing only. Being valued. Vulnerability is the stepping stone that helps us to achieve that goal. Hence there is power in vulnerability because not only are we saying, "Hey you're my person that I'm trusting with the most delicate parts of me but I'm also brave enough to dig out all the parts of me that's pretty, scary, and ugly that I might not even like."

It reminds me of a conversation I once had with a young woman. She was beautiful, full of life, came from a home where she never had to want for anything, and at a young age got a chance to travel the world. We talked at length about relationships and love. She mentioned to me that she was never in love but did experience loving someone and asked me the difference between both.

Though the question was a no brainer for me, it got me thinking about vulnerability and love. Love requires us to open ourselves up to the possibility of vulnerability despite the fear of being hurt and disappointed. But does the door to vulnerability seal itself shut after we've been disappointed so many times? Is it possible to seal off vulnerability?

I think we all have the ability to be vulnerable but when we're disappointed over and over again we have a choice. Do we allow these pains to dictate our position of vulnerability or do we continue on in strength? Vulnerability is a choice, it's a fluid free-forming decision that we make in a split second.

Going back to the conversation with the young woman, at the end of our conversation she says to me, "How come every relationship you've been in your significant other is always like your best friend?" My answer because no matter how many times I've been knocked down, disappointed, and hurt I still choose vulnerability.

I choose to have deep meaningful relationships that rock my soul. I strive for conversations, and moments in life that get me to think, learn, and sincerely feel authenticity in it's the rarest form.

***

If we're talking about vulnerability here's an honest moment, too often I've struggled with success. You see I was taught a different picture of what success looks like. In fact, growing up I idealized success thinking that it was strictly having a lot of money and traveling the world.

Though that can be a part of success as I've outgrown that notion I started to realize something. Success is simply what we deem it as. Not every definition of success is a good one but no every definition is a bad one either. For many many years people would often say to me, "Wow you're so successful, how did you do it?" My default response is always, "It's a whole lot of tears, sweat equity, falling flat on your face, and getting back up again." What I was feeling on the inside was and still is, I don't feel successful because I haven't reached the pinnacle of what success feels like to me.

Success can come in so many forms, we can be successful in our relationships, with our emotions, in our business, mastering ourselves as a parent, etc. Look no one's perfect so there isn't a "perfect" definition of what success is. In fact, success is freedom because YOU get to define it on your terms and you can always change the picture at any time.

Success and vulnerability become your worth as a person, in part, it's your contribution to the world, the value that you give out and receive. Though it's human nature to want or sometimes even require a definite guiding post. It's this obsessive requirement for something tangible that's the reason why we consistently have a "picture" of how success looks like. We search for a way to measure things to make sure it's working or we're on the right path. Instead I'd encourage you to flip that and ask yourself how does success FEEL like? Change the definition and you change the outcome.

As I mentioned before vulnerability is a choice, being that it's so, we can continuously choose to stay open to vulnerability, deepening our connection to each other or closed off to the world and suffer quietly in loneliness.

We are the designers of our lives and vulnerability is the gateway to creativity. It opens us up to endless possibilities on how to creatively design our own lives, leaving the control in our hands. It gives us the child-like ability to imagine and reimagine the possibilities. When we live with child-like curiosity you get to soak in life, learn, grow our minds, and even expand. The beauty of this is that it creates a habit of compassion learning.

Compassion is another output of vulnerability, it allows us to say, "I see you, I feel you and I understand you." But let me tell you it's probably the hardest to put into practice especially when someone does you wrong. In that moment your primitive brain kicks in and develops a fight or flight response. Let's be real, someone puts you down, calls you out your name. I promise you that in that moment you're absolutely not thinking, "Oh yes, I feel you, I hear you and I understand you." Quite the opposite you're probably ready to go into fight mode, verbal assassinations, or even borderline losing your sanity.

It takes being vulnerable with yourself first before you can reach a point that you can circumvent situations that would trigger the primitive side of your brain. By being grounded, knowing your weaknesses you start to really work on strengthening yourself. When it comes to weaknesses, proudly own them it's the surest way to protect against the judgement of others. Though we are all imperfect people but when you own even your weaknesses it gives you power. The power to know that no matter what people say about you that you have full control over it. Striking the balance between the two worlds enables us to hold our heads high as we journey through.

Owning your vulnerability is a way that we hold ourselves accountable and responsible for our own actions. It's not enough to live in a world of let's wish and see what happens. In fact when we are reckless with our actions and behaviors we end up hurting the ones who we love the most. The daily practice of responsibility is something that needs to become a habitual part of our lives in order to cultivate meaningful and deep relationships that change our lives.

SECRET 3: HARNESS YOUR POWER

Within us lies a power that can't be described in words nor can it be replicated because that power you possess is unique to you and your abilities. Each one of us has a special power, skill set and character traits that make us who we are. In order to continuously harness our power we need to learn. Learning is something we do till we die and I'm not talking about learning in school. Though that's one aspect of learning but it's also a very limited scope of education that was devised during a time when life was much different.

I encourage you to be curious about things. It doesn't matter how big or small, but get into the habit of learning and researching. If someone talks about something that you don't know what it means, Google it. I've come to believe that information is simply at our fingertips and it's just a matter of asking the right questions.

Questions don't make you look like a fool, instead asking questions is for yourself. It's a way to demonstrate how you think and helps you reshape your beliefs. Aside from being a business owner I also mentor teen entrepreneurs. They are a group of people whom I'm passionate about helping because they are the next generation who will carry the torch. When I mentor these teens I always encourage them to think outside the box and cheer them on to be bold in their approach.

Many times the awe in their voice is what moves me, it's like their minds just opened up to a new way of looking at things. That moment is what I live for and why I mentor teen entrepreneurs. These teens also challenge me on an emotional plane as they are all highly curious about life. I encourage you to be like these teens when it comes to curiosity and dare to ask why.

Too often we get comfortable to the point where we stop asking the questions that matter. This is the space where people end up dying at least on an emotional front. You see this often when people are busy chasing materialistic things. They are also the same ones that want to "floss" and post cash, cars, boats on social media. Stay away from those types of people. If you really look at the ballers out there, the Bill Gates of the world, they're definitely not posting or even speaking about money all the time.

Matter of fact the wealthiest people in the world don't focus on money instead they're focusing on how they give back to the world and make society a better place. When you take your internal power and you focus it on helping others to inspire the world, money will come to you.

It's about shifting the way you're operating. We were taught that it takes money to make money. Yes that's true but it's also true that you can be financially wealthy but spiritually deficient. Read it again, *financially wealthy but spiritually deficient.*

You can have all the money in the world but if you're not using that money for a force of good then it doesn't mean anything to be "rich". Wealth and richness needs to be a well-rounded approach, it's a balance. Have the money and also have the ability to help others or even change the world, leave it better than the way you found it.

***

Oftentimes the power we yield, we give it away to someone else. Allowing someone else to make us feel small or even less than are the perfect examples of giving away our power. You need to remember that someone can not take away your power without your permission. Our power is our energy and you need to be selective about who we dispense it to. Not everyone deserves your power and energy. Heck not everyone will even understand your power and energy. But that should not stop you from still giving your 100 percent energy to things that are meaningful to us.

The more we give away our power the less we have to serve the world and live fulfilled lives because we're so busy filling up someone else's cup. In fact we need to practice how to harness our power, create a balance of give and take. This is where you need to use sound judgement to determine what instances you should hold back and when you should give. This also applies to business.

The key to business is knowing which opportunities to say yes to and which ones you need to say no to. It took me years of practice to understand that when I say yes to every business opportunity that I'm also giving away my power. Not every opportunity is going to be worth your time. Recently I spent a whole day saying no to opportunities as a reminder of what it feels like to hold onto my power.

What was amazing was not only did I turn down so many opportunities but it made me feel like I was controlling more of my energy. I can't stress enough how important it is to learn to say no without worrying about offending someone or feeling guilty. These opportunities I turned down were vetted by bumping them against what was on my plate and how I intuitively felt before I determined they were a hard pass.

In the past when I said, "yes" to every opportunity and partnership, those were the same projects that ended up draining me and it took weeks to recover. Some of these opportunities didn't even pay me but I gained tons of experiences in exchange for my energy. My goal is to share with you what I did wrong so that you can avoid it and create your own methodology on power harnessing.

I talk alot about balance because it's crucial to staying grounded. A word of caution, when we realize how much power we hold, it can tether us to be on the edge of being power hungry or develop into power trips. Know that power trips are the ego's way of talking to you, so in this instant you must learn to check yourself. There's nothing sexy about being power hungry, in fact it just shows that you're not spiritually developed.

Having power doesn't mean that you control the people around you. Matter of fact true power is mastering your own inner world and emotions. That's true power! What's most impressive is when you can get to a point where you aren't reactive to every situation in life no matter what emotion it conjures up within. Trust me it's not easy. I'm still learning and at times I have to catch myself too.

Our power is our beauty, it's our unique non-verbal fingerprint that shows who we are without using words. Learn to harness your power, don't give it away nilly willy and definitely know when to give and take. Stay in your power, you owe it to yourself to honor YOU!

SECRET 4: GUILT IS A DIRTY WORD

Let's talk about the salacious G word- GUILT! Guilt has this way of creeping up on us in the most inconvenient times. You might be on a roll and all of a sudden feeling guilty about something that's just silly. It used to happen to me all the time to the point where it paralyzed me from making decisions. The thing about guilt is this, dwell on it long enough and it quickly snowballs into fear. Then we start blaming ourselves for all kinds of things.

If you're anything like me, an extreme overachiever, you might have some sort of internal guilt dialogue that comes with a mental checklist justifying the guilt. Funny thing is when we get into this mode we never blame ourselves for the good things that happen. It always seems to be bad. Have you noticed that?

The problem with guilt is that it throws us off our game. It's definitely responsible for resentment, belabored self-punishment and a whole slew of things including the inability to enjoy life. I used to feel guilty about a lot of things. For one happiness, somehow I believed in that I didn't deserve happiness and that life was about suffering.

Once I started to create my own lane through my businesses, my newly discovered epiphany was that happiness is the sweet nectar of life. That life should be lived in a constant state of happiness and joy. I lived life on the other side, had a comparison and realized how much happiness can change your whole world. Look I'm not saying that starting a business will help alleviate guilt. For some it won't, for me it opened my eyes- I was "woke."

Guilt also has this way of making us play small because we get engulfed in the feeling and it morphs into all kinds of ugly. As a byproduct we're living small, playing small and unable to get creative and live outside the box. It then becomes our safety net and we start to believe that it will protect us against unknown evils. In fact, life isn't meant to live small, if that were true we wouldn't see some of the most inspiring people making a huge difference in the world.

Did you know that there was a study that found we spend 5 hours a week feeling guilty? For fun, let's just do the math, 5 hours of weekly guilt equals 20 hours accumulated in a month. Now in a year we spend 240 hours feeling guilty- that's a lot of hours! Imagine if we used those extra hours to find happiness or do things that will impact humanity, what would the world look like?

Now spending 240 hours a year feeling guilty is the ultimate definition of giving ourselves a guilt trip. When we're guilt tripping we become resentful. Resentful of things for the wrong reasons and even of people. It tends to leave us living in a space of negativity. Is that a conducive space you want to live in? I'm betting no right?

So how do we get past guilt? For one, you are HUMAN! It means that you'll make mistakes. Mistakes are teachable moments, learning opportunities that make us better people. Instead of stewing in guilt take it as an opportunity to do better next time. This is also your chance to reimagine what a guilt-free future would look like. Get creative, fantasize and give yourself the permission to thoughtfully wander. Pay attention to what makes you feel guilty and make a conscious effort to catch yourself when the emotion comes up.

It'll take some practice but with time you'll be able to minimize guilt. I'm not saying you'll completely eradicate guilt but at least the 240 hours a year will dwindle. Truth be told it doesn't matter how long you indulge guilt it doesn't change the fact that the event already occurred. There's no turning back time but there is a chance for you to be better by forgiving yourself.

We hold ourselves to an unforgiving standard and don't allow grace for our mistakes. The art of forgiveness is not just for others but it's also learning how to forgive YOU! Forgiving your guilt doesn't mean that you're giving it a hard pass. No, matter of fact you're just allowing yourself room for error. We need to make mistakes and experience the range of emotions. I mean how else will we grow?

I believe that experiences are the flavor of life. They open our eyes to new possibilities and a different way of living. With every new experience we go through it changes us. In some ways it could change us for the best or maybe even for the worse. Regardless of which direction your ship sails it's these experiences that carry us to the next level in life, like a video game. Experience is what helps us gain wisdom, clarity and even reshape our beliefs.

Speaking of experiences, in the past the idea of making a lot of money made me feel guilty because there's so many out there who are struggling on a day to day basis. During my corporate stint I won't lie, I made very good money working in the luxury industry. As a 20 something year old making six figures it was definitely jaw-dropping. Not just that I was in a highly lucrative and coveted industry-diamonds.

Being in that kind of environment I saw diamonds being exchanged with a handshake, massive vaults built like fortresses stacked with stones from top to bottom, and expansive trade shows the size of 2-3 football fields filled with diamonds from all over the world. I saw uncut stones, cut stones, and even insanely large diamonds passed through my own hands. Seeing an internally flawless diamond was a daily norm, my heart never skipped a beat. Heck wearing a 108 carat diamond necklace around my neck with 4 carat diamond stud earrings onto a commercial flight didn't make me flinch and I didn't travel with a bodyguard.

So you can only imagine the tremendous amount of guilt I felt. Guilt aside it was definitely fun being in that industry, experiencing things that many would never have gotten the chance to. At the time I was traveling often and every paycheck I had was spent on either expensive handbags, fine dining, or expensive wines.

I would justify my guilt by spending as much of my money as possible because when I spent the money it felt like I was sharing the wealth. I shared the wealth so much that one day I woke up realizing that feeling guilty about making money was making me unhappy even kind of angry.

Back then I probably spent more hours feeling guilty than happy. Have you ever gotten tired of feeling tired about something? Well that's exactly what happened to me and it motivated me to start my own businesses. In the beginning it was touch and go but the guilt was still there. This time I felt guilty about deserting my corporate job. But as you keep going through different wins on your journey you start to reshape your lens and how you look at things.

It'll never be perfect but the whole point is to be proactive in satiating guilt and kiboshing the internal guilt checklist. I assure you that navigating guilt you're going to bob and weave, revert back to your old ways and even come up with new things to be guilty about. The most important part is to give yourself grace.

SECRET 5: GET A SQUAD

"Friendship is born at that moment when one person says to another, 'What! You too? I thought I was the only one.'" C.S. Lewis

This right here says it all. On our life journey it's so important to find a squad of people who will cheer you on. Friendships are supposed to be meaningful, not just people who you can go to the club with or grab drinks. These are people who must bring value to your life.

At every juncture of our lives we're going to need different people and a different circle. Having friends who you can just "hang" with is great but if you're looking to have deeply robust connections that challenge you to grow, then get better friends. You might have a friend who will always give you level-headed advice while another friend is there for emotional support.

Our friendships say a lot about who we are and at what point of life we're in. The people you choose to spend the most amount of time with shouldn't be those encouraging you to follow the "herd" mentality. Or encouraging you to post everything about your life on Tik Tok and Instagram. Matter of fact they have to be the ones who not only challenge you but also call you out on your BS.

As someone who is a business owner, it's really hard to find people who get what you're doing and why you're relentlessly chasing dreams. My friendship circle has dwindled down to 3 solid people who I can call on for life advice. I know it doesn't sound like a lot, but these 3 people are the ones that I can turn to for support whether it's on the business front or on the personal front. They are also the ones who tell me when I need to get it together or have a softer approach to things.

Being a female business owner it's even more important to surround yourself with other female business owners. Why? Women lead companies in a very unique way that's different from men. We not only lead with intention, wisdom, and tenacity but we also bring in our feminine energy. For those of you who don't believe in energies, I'm telling you now it's very real and it's what connects us all.

Women who run businesses have to be able to pull their weight in a room full of men. But when we're in that environment constantly we start to adapt a masculine energy. So that's why it's important to have friends who are also female business owners to balance you out.

When picking your friends you need to be highly selective. Pay attention to their value system, what do they believe in and what do they stand for. Notice the language and words that they are using. Are they constantly using negative verbiage or are they speaking positively with support? Use your intuition to determine if they are genuine or not. All these things impact you so select wisely.

I always pay attention to people's body language and their subconscious intentions. For example if I notice that someone is a nail biter I won't allow that person into my circle. I know it sounds judgy but let me explain why. Someone who is a nail biter is a person who either lacks confidence or has a ton of nervous energy. Running a business I already spend a lot of time going emotionally up and down so the last thing I need is to have someone's nervous energy in my space.

The other thing I also pay attention to is someone's eyes. As the saying goes, "eyes are the window to the soul," that is quite true. When someone is speaking, look into their eyes and it'll tell you a lot about a person. Simply by doing this you can tell if someone is serious, malicious, shady, genuine, has been hurt before, etc. There's a whole set of things you learn about someone simply through eye contact. I know this might be getting a bit too deep, but this is your life we're talking about. Choose your friends with intention and allow yourself to learn about people, pay attention.

When it comes to friendships, know that not everyone is destined to stay in your life forever. Sometimes people are meant to stay for a season to teach you something and leave. Don't hold onto friends that have past their expiration date, you're only hurting yourself in the long run. If people choose to leave your life, wish them well and keep it on moving. It does sound sad but you need to make room for better friends to come into the next cycle of your life. If we keep holding onto those friendships that don't bring value we're basically letting them take up space for someone else who is much better or more compatible with our next life cycle.

Long time ago I used to have a lot of friends. Everywhere I went there was someone I knew and they knew me. It doesn't matter if it was at a restaurant, bar, or even professional settings. Each one of these individuals were the same people in a different body. They were simply there to just "hang" out with or they were the ones that you could always call on at the last minute to grab a drink. Trust me at the time I thought that was what friendship looked like. It was until I started to notice that if I took out alcohol from the equation, I really had nothing in common with any one of them.

Our conversations were filled with complaints about our bosses, family life, bills or lack of money. It was mindless chit chat to just pass the time and there was no value. I mean let's keep it real. How many ways can you say that you can't stand your job? Eventually those conversations tired me out. I wasn't even happy anymore talking to people, matter of fact it made me cringe. I needed more depth in conversations, more challenging conversations that made me think. I started to look for a new circle.

In the beginning it was lonely because I couldn't find the type of friends that would fulfill what I was looking for. It was until I entered into the real estate world. That's when I was introduced to high level individuals who thought differently who moved differently. Like that my world changed! These were the types of people I wanted to be around, go-getters, sharp, sharks, and knew what they wanted from life.

From then on I never looked back because today my small circle of friends are just like that. They are all unapologetically powerful in their own right. They operate on a level that isn't like many people. So when I say intentionally pick your friends this is why. Your friends can impact your thought process, your life trajectory and even your immediate environment. It's simply done through the flow of energetic exchanges.

Going through this experience has taught me to quickly identify if this is someone I want to be in my life. I've gotten so good at it that within seconds I can basically make that determination. On top of that I can feel their emotions and intentions. It takes practice but I assure you if you pay attention to all these little details you can get good at this too.

I want you to remember to never be in a room where you are the smartest person. Never! If you're the smartest person in that room you are in the wrong room. Every experience that we have in life should be a learning opportunity. If you're the smartest person in the room then what exactly are you going to learn that don't already know? This isn't about being a snob but in fact it's about gaining knowledge to level YOU up, to make you grow. We can learn from everyone but if you want to expand your mind, be around those who will challenge you in a good way to think differently.

Set your squad goals high, you deserve it. We need friendships in our lives so don't read this and take it as a sign to isolate yourself. Isolation is not the answer because it can damage our spirit and mental well-being. We're built to connect but I'm just saying plug your battery wisely.

This means that if you are a battery console and looking to recharge you don't want to plug into an outlet that is not compatible. It's like you're an American appliance trying to plug into a European electric outlet. We all know that it won't fit. Treat your friendships the same way, find the right outlet to charge and recharge.

SECRET 6: FORGIVENESS

Forgiveness is an artform that took me nearly fifteen years to understand. As kids our parents tell us to forgive other kids who have done us wrong and say, "Sorry." Though it was something we were always taught but never did anyone tell me as an adult it's an artform and mastering it sans ego is HARD AF! Here's the brutal truth, though I'm writing a book about being a better human, even today I struggle with forgiveness.

The biggest challenge is always forgiving yourself. No matter how prepared you are or how knowledgeable you are about people and situations you are never fully prepared when it comes to other people because human behavior is always a variable. People's actions and behaviors can hurt you and you're left to pick up the pieces. As an entrepreneur I've had to make tons of split second decisions and judgement calls.

I'd like to think that I'm pretty good at this but unfortunately there are still instances where I find myself asking myself, "didn't you see that coming a mile away?" Here's the deal: I'm certified in neurolinguistic programming (NLP), been through hell and back, lost 3 companies, certified in a bunch of things, wrote two books, and so much more. I say all this not to tout but to say that even after all these accolades I still make mistakes. Sometimes I made judgement calls I thought were right at the time and they turned out to be the worst ideas. Or believing in someone's potential and they let me down numerous times.

As painful as these experiences were, the recovery part isn't as easy because this is where you need to implement the artform of forgiveness. It's not enough to forgive someone in words but forgiving them in thought and emotions is the trickiest.

Remember I told you I went to hell and back? Well if you're wondering how bad it was, here's the story. Many years ago I had gotten into the wrong relationship with a man who I thought the world of. Did I love him? Yes. But the relationship ended violently and I almost lost my life in his hands literally.

That was one of the scariest moments in my life, especially when I found myself praying to GOD for this man to just kill me. It's an eye opening experiencing when you're under that kind of duress and literally praying for death. I'll spare you the gorey details but long story short the road to recovery was harrowing and long.

I spent a year in therapy and had to learn what it meant to forgive myself. You know in therapy they always tell you that it's not your fault. As much as I wanted to believe it, I was troubleshooting how it couldn't have been my fault for not seeing the signs. It gets dangerous when we repeatedly punish ourselves for the actions of others. We start to question our worth and the possibility of whether we are of sound mind and spirit.

During that time the one burning question I had was how do I forgive someone who almost killed me? Look I'm no Mother Teresa nor am I anywhere close to being saintly. It's a question I struggled with until one day I met a priest.

As I walked the streets of Philadelphia while attending a seminar on spirituality I spotted a priest from across the street. At that moment I was determined to bee-line it straight to him and ask the question, "how do you forgive someone who almost kills you." I thought it was the best idea ever. Why? One a priest is the holiest of holies and a wise sage. Two, I will never see him again and he doesn't know who I am. Three he's obligated to answer my question, he is a priest after all.

I pulled back my shoulders and confidently crossed the street as I approached him, he looked at me as though he knew I was coming in hot and determined. I said, "Excuse me Father, I wanted to ask you a question. How do you forgive someone who almost kills you?" Looking back at it I obviously didn't employ much tack or couth. I probably should've better prefaced my question because in a split section he was alarmed and I had to elaborate where the question was coming from.

He looked at me and calmly replied, "You just do." My overachiever entrepreneur brain thought what do you mean you just do? It can't be that easy! NO WAY! I was expecting him to give me a forgiveness blueprint, some sort of spiritual step by step guide with a follow up action plan. We entrepreneurs have a thing about blueprints and data. The priest offered me none of that.

Clearly he saw my confusion and went on to tell me a story about a drunk driver who mowed down and killed a young man while he was crossing the street. At the court sentencing the young man's mother stood up to speak and asked the judge for leniency. Part of her plea she said to the drunk driver, "Even though I lost a son, I want you to know that I still forgive you. We as humans all make mistakes and I want you to forgive yourself as I have forgiven you." Shocked? Me too! It's one of those stories that will stick with you for life.

After hearing that I spent a lot of time contemplating how in my own way I was going to forgive not just myself but also the person who almost killed me. In instances like this one you grapple with the reality of anger versus forgiveness. I meditated on it, prayed on it and even cried about it because part of me didn't want to let go of my anger but I knew my spirit needed me to do better.

How did I finally come to forgive this person? Truth, I spent countless hours and months sending this person love. Do you know how difficult that is? I did it through meditation and kept telling myself that this person isn't equipped for life and needs love. I prayed a couple hundreds of times in a span of a year asking GOD to send him love and forgive him. In the beginning I did this begrudgingly but as time went on something happened.

I started to find peace within myself and let me tell you, that peace of mind and heart is so much more comforting than holding onto anger. Within the process I've learned to forgive and love myself -the most important person in the equation here. For the first time I was able to understand that forgiveness isn't really for the other person but selfishly it's for ourselves and that too is ok. Forgive yourself for being selfish, you earned the right.

Now after going through all that you'd figure I would be a forgiveness pro right? Not at all I still do struggle with it and just like vulnerability it's a daily practice. There are times that I want to scream and stomp my feet, revert back to caveman days but have to remind myself that I am an evolved woman. One who has the strength to overcome even the toughest adversities while strangers stand guard in judgement of my every action and every word. As they dissect the underlying meaning of why I said something or hang onto my every word as though it was gold.

Own your mistakes, your bad judgements and even the unforgiving parts of yourself. I promise you only good comes out of it. Plus it's easier to live that way. I'm not saying that the process of forgiveness is going to be packaged in a pretty bow with nice wrapping paper.

The harsh reality is that forgiveness is sloppy, raw, and definitely not a pretty process. For me I'll be the first to admit that I'm a major crier, that's me owning it. I'm the type of person who can watch the movie Transformers and manage to cry when Bumblee got destroyed. Bumblebee for your information is a car.

You'll go through moments where you have uncontrollable tears and moments where you feel like superwoman and can take on the world. Enjoy each of these moments, they teach you to be better, to lead with compassion, empathy and vulnerability in the most authentic ways. Channel that energy to help serve the world and inspire others who don't necessarily have the courage to forgive or who haven't mastered that art of forgiveness. Indeed it sounds like an insurmountable task and heavy with responsibilities but you owe it to yourself.

If forgiveness did come in a pretty package, it wouldn't be called forgiveness because it would be staged. It would be someone else's version of what forgiveness is supposed to mean. In fact forgiveness is a personalized approach, we forgive people for many different reasons whether they are big or small. Whether they have deeply scarred us or not. There are even times that we forgive someone without them even knowing it. I've done that infinite times. No matter how you forgive there isn't a right or wrong way to do it. But there is an authentic and fake way. If you're just saying you forgive someone I want you to know that it's a start but it doesn't wholeheartedly count just yet as full blown genuine forgiveness.

SECRET 7: BELIEVE IT OR NOT

Show me don't tell me. I'm cut from the old school cloth of "your word is bond," and I do what I say and say what I do. It's part of living a life with integrity. In today's world it's a rare find, many people will say almost anything to get you to bend to their convenience. Look at sleazy salespeople and marketers, they know exactly what to say or what copy to use in ads to get customers to buy. They know how to tap into emotions with precision.

Heck it's even prevalent when it comes to dating. People will say anything just to portray themselves in the best light. But how someone behaves is the ultimate tell, I'd trust behavior more. I'll go even one step further to say that I would trust how people are behaving when no one is looking. That is a person's true nature.

It's easy to believe in all those nice things that people say but what are their intentions behind the words. I've been trained to listen to people's subconscious language rather than the surface words and behavior. This is one of those things that's a blessing and a curse because sometimes their subconscious intent is malicious.

Surface behavior can be manipulated, a perfect example is acting. Actors know how to get into character with a drop of a dime. Cry on command and even recreate love chemistry on screen instantly to make it believable to the audience. Don't get me wrong, I'm not dogging anyone in the acting world here, just using the profession to prove a point.

As you get older and wiser you start to subscribe to the notion of show me don't tell me. An easy example that I think we can all relate to is dating and courtship. During this phase if someone tells you that they love you but behind your back they're flirting with other people or entertaining other options does that person really love you? In fact I believe they are showing you otherwise. Their behavior and words aren't a match. In this instant believe their behavior.

Instead if the person truly loves you, you would be their priority; they would treat you with the highest level of respect and integrity. They would say, "I love you," and their behavior would represent that in all areas including the way they interact with others behind your back. You will always be top of mind.

They wouldn't flirt with someone else, you would be their priority, they might even commit to you, etc. You get the point I'm making here, your words need to have integrity behind it. Integrity can't be faked; it's either you have it or don't.

Having worked in the diamond industry for so long, I learned the value of integrity and how crucial it is to honor your word. For many years I've watched millions of dollars worth of diamond sales done with simply a handshake. Though in today's business world experts and lawyers will tell you that is bad business etiquette. But in the diamond world it's something that is sacred. Your worth and reputation lies within that one handshake.

All we have in this world is our name and reputation. It's true, it takes a lifetime to build a reputation but it can be destroyed in 5 minutes. Yes, you can say "I don't care what people think of me." But I think the better question to ask is, do you care what you think of you? Can you look yourself in the mirror knowing you were sleazy?

Success in life starts with the small things. Simple acts become habits and habits become character. If you change simple behavioral patterns then you start to set yourself up for a different kind of life. A life that's meaningful and purposeful.

An integral part of life is to have purpose rather than just throwing shit to the wall and seeing what sticks. It's easy to implement that latter strategy, most people are doing that in today's society, it's the easy way out. Just look around and you'll see how many people are chasing clout, followers, and likes on social media or spending every open minute with their noises glued to a small screen in their hands.

You need to be purposeful and strategically plan the moves you make. It's just like in business where you have to play mental chess against yourself and the world. Recently I discovered the concept of "Thinking Time," as Keith J. Cunningham coins it. The idea is to spend 45 minutes without any distraction, interruptions and think. You write down a question that you want to work through. It can be any question. In those 45 minutes you write down every solution that comes to mind, sort of like a brain dump session with yourself.

I've used this process for my personal life and my business. Let me tell you it's magical because each time you're done it gives you so much clarity. We need clarity to better understand our life's direction and to create better life strategies.

Our words hold tremendous weight and when we operate with meaningless words that lack integrity we don't attract the right people and opportunities into our lives. If your goal is to level up in life then start by building integrity- it's your foundation.

SECRET 8: THE FINAL DIRTY SECRET

Our lives are filled with endless possibilities, opportunities, hopes and dreams. No matter which path you choose to take, remember that you are the designer of your life. The good and the bad are part of it and it doesn't make you a failure or anymore less than the next person. We all have our strengths and struggles so be kind to one another.

This lifetime is gifted to you, without you asking for it. It means you have the most precious chance to make it special, customize it so that you can be a productive individual to society. A society where change is much needed, where innovation can make lives better and it's going to be your creativity that paves the way for our next generation to have the courage to strive for better.

We weren't all given courage, we learned to be courageous no matter what happened to us in life. Your moments and heartbreaks taught you to be resilient, strong and not give up on the things you truly believe in.

My wish for you is that you choose to continue to be courageous, to live outside the box and have the strength to be a free spirit. A spirit that isn't afraid to embrace the overachiever within you even when the odds are stacked against you or when hope is dim. Each and every one of us are born to create. We were given life to make a difference in the world. The impact that we create no matter how small or big is a ripple effect that changes all of us.

I want you to be brave enough to lend your voice to those who haven't found theirs and bold enough to inspire others in ways that quenches the soul's thirst. Above all, have faith because our faith will carry us beyond the winds, giving us the sheer power to hope for a better future, a better life, and even a better world.

OVERACHIEVING FINAL THOUGHTS

In life to attain the unattainable we must always strive to be the best version of ourselves, setting standards that others might see as impossible. We are given this one life to achieve greatness in whatever capacity we are destined for. Whatever life choices you make remember that there are two sides to every decision. The good and the bad.

We can all handle when good things happen but in true overachiever form you need to also look at the bad. One of the lessons I learned as a business owner is this, always ask yourself can I handle the bad outcome in one year, five years or even ten years. If the answer is no then don't hedge that bet.

It isn't about saying yes to everything or even accepting anything that comes your way. Aim high on the goalpost of life. Keep your standards high in everything you do and no matter what DO NOT ever lower your standard to fit into someone else's frame or story. This is YOUR life, your story, and if you aren't keeping yourself accountable then you can forget about accomplishing greatness.

It's our standards and integrity that challenge us to be better people, better contributors to society. Aside from a business owner, I'm also a publicist to many high level talents. To my surprise some of them look beyond successful on the outside but on the inside they lack standards. It's always puzzling to me why such successful people don't take more care to hold steady to their standards. It's one of those mysteries in life that I will probably never know the answer to and I'm okay with that.

But I digress, standards aren't the only thing that is important to us overachievers. If you study overachievers you'll discover that they have this built in, innate emotional need to succeed. That drive can't be taught and it's not something someone hands you. It's something within us that is like oxygen. That innate need to succeed is driven by their value system. Most overachievers have a high value system that is their operational blueprint.

To many people having high standards, innate emotional need to succeed, and a high value system seems like it's a lot of work. But this is the lifestyle of an individual who overachieves.

We need strong foundations to build our dreams and it starts from within. When we have clarity it's magical because you know exactly what, where and how we're going to accomplish our goals. For me I knew in my 20's that I was destined for something great. Even though no one believed in me I had to learn to believe in myself, cheer myself on and figure it out.

In writing this book it started as a cathartic experience for me to share my experiences and put my thoughts to paper for clarity. But as I continued to clank away on the keyboard I realized that many people are wondering how to achieve success. What is the secret?

Look there's no secret to success, I promise you. In fact you'll fall on your face, have embarrassing moments, and times that you wish you could take things back. Success starts as an inside job. No one is handing out wins like sample tastings so it's up to you to create your lane. Before you start listing out all the things you want and the goals you want to attain in life I strongly suggest you do the inside homework of growth, don't skip a page either.

Be honest with yourself where you are lacking, what mistakes have you made and are repeating over and over again. What values do you need to get rid of and how are you living according to your value system? I did the homework and to be honest, I'm still doing it. Everyday is something new that I didn't know about myself or didn't even realize was within me. I'm constantly analyzing myself in the third person as though I was having an out of body experience.

What I want for you is to be a well-rounded overachiever. Don't make the mistake of having a one lane tunnel vision. Allow yourself to expand your mind, think about things from various points of view and practice living with integrity in all areas of life. Create a picture of what success looks like to you because everyone's definition is different. But I will tell you this success is not having a million dollars in the bank or owning multiple real estate properties. It's so much more than that.

You can have the materialist stuff and still be a jerk. The world doesn't need more jerks so that's why I'm here to tell you that you need to find a balance that works for you. It doesn't matter what you've already been through in life, that's the past. Everyday we wake up and have the opportunity to create a new vision for ourselves, a new story.

It's up to you if you have the courage to live out that new story. Are you brave enough for change or are you just willing to shout it out on the rooftops? My story to success isn't some mind blowing hack. It took me 6 years to start my first company, 16 years to find my happiness, 5 years to land my first TEDx Talk, and many more years of countless accomplishments big and small. My youth wasn't perfect; it was filled with living on the edge, but I have stories, experiences and memories that I learned from.

I want you to know that being an overachiever isn't a bad thing. Become the best version of who you are whether it's your career, entrepreneurship, parent, woman, man, husband, wife, etc. Along the way, I hope that you overachieve your failures as much as you overachieve your wins. It's in our moments of failures that we grow the most, learn the best lessons in life and guess what? Those are the moments that not only define us but also makes us unique.

Your failures are never really failures and you didn't experience them in vain. Each failure is to be looked at as a learning experience, teachable moment. There's no good that will come of it if you dwell on your failures reliving them day in and day out. Matter of fact I'd welcome you to remove the word failure from your vocabulary all together, along with the word problems.

Our self talk can make or break us. If we are looking to build a better life, change how you're talking to yourself. The intimate conversations we are having with ourselves affect how we think and lead. If you aren't changing your mind how will you change the world? When it comes to overachieving your mistakes and challenges I want you to vehemently learn, take notes and connect the dots. This is part of doing the work that others aren't willing to do.

On this journey whether you are an entrepreneur or not remember that YOU have to fight for your dreams. It's our dreams that give us purpose and inspiration. Use your imagination in every which way, dream the impossible. Every invention in the world started with a dream and a curiosity question. Mankind dared to dream an impossible dream and then had the audacity to turn it into reality.

One of my favorite things is having the ability to create something from nothing. In my life there have been and will continue to be ideas that come up and I turn them into reality. I've watched this manifest itself over and over again in sheer amazement. Each time it happens it gives me the confidence to dream even bigger. I get to challenge who I was yesterday and what I will accomplish.

So before we part ways I want to encourage you to go forth and overachieve the shit out of life, I will be here cheering you on.

ABOUT THE AUTHOR

Connie Chi is an expert in media communications, public speaker, and founder of The Chi Group, an award-winning PR and brand management agency working with inspirational talents, personalities, and brands. She speaks across the United States about public relations, marketing, brand management, media communications, entrepreneurship, and is known for her TEDx Talk titled, *"Lonely AF: Lonely About Failure."* Chi has been featured in Business Insider, Yahoo Finance, Thrive Global, Reader's Digest, Vain Culture, Authority Magazine and many more media outlets.

Her robust background includes being certified in Neurolinguistic Programming (NLP), GIA Diamond Grading, and Event PLanning. She has over 18 years of combined experience in luxury marketing, public relations, brand management, branding, and sales working alongside global brands such as: Nielsen, 99 Ranch, Lord & Taylor, Reebok, Van Cleef & Arpels, Bailey Banks & Biddle, Fortunoff and many more.

For more information about The Chi Group visit www.thechigroup.co Interested in having Connie speak at your next event or for press interviews please contact

press@thechigroup.co